IN MY UNDERSTANDING

This prymer of Salysbury use...

God be in my hede
  And in myn understandynge
God be in myn eyen
  And in my lokynge
God be in my mouth
  And in myn spekynge
God be in my herte
  And in my thynkynge
God be at myn ende
  And at my departynge.

GEORGE SIMMS

In my Understanding

Gill and Macmillan

First published 1982 by
Gill and Macmillan Ltd
Goldenbridge
Dublin 8
with associated companies in
London, New York, Delhi, Hong Kong,
Johannesburg, Lagos, Melbourne,
Singapore, Tokyo

7171 1103 2

The frontispiece is reproduced by kind permission of
the Governors and Guardians of Marsh's Library

Origination by A.D.C. Ltd., 56 Pembroke Road, Dublin 4.

Printed and bound in Great Britain by
Biddles Ltd., Guildford and King's Lynn

To M.F.S.
in gratitude

'God be in my hede
and in myn understandynge
God be in myn eyen
and in my lokynge
God be in my mouth
and in my spekynge
God be in my herte
and in my thynkynge
God be at myn ende
and at my departynge'

(author unknown, origin uncertain,
in use in fifteenth century, in Sarum Primer)

Contents

Introduction

The prayer printed on the title page of the 'prymer of Salysbury' reminds us that Rouen shared with Paris almost a monopoly in the printing of Books of Hours. The name Rouen and the early date in the history of printing, 1538, appear on this page.

Sarum, the Latin name for Salisbury, gave its name to the local modification of the Roman rite in the medieval Church. This Sarum use was widely popular and there were many reprints of it. A complete directory of services was compiled by Richard le Poore, dean of Salisbury, in 1237; while the new use of Sarum was a further fourteenth-century revision, with certain changes in the calendar. In the later Middle Ages the Sarum order was increasingly followed in other dioceses, and in 1457 was stated to be in use in nearly the whole of England, Wales and Ireland. The books of the Sarum rite provided the Reformers with their main material for the Book of Common Prayer in 1549. In that first Book of Edward VI the Sarum rite is mentioned in the preface, 'Concerning the Service of the Church'. Sarum was outstanding among the five uses referred to, the other four being Hereford, Bangor, York and Lincoln. Sarum is responsible for the style 'Sundays after Trinity' rather than 'Sundays after Pentecost'.

'The 'prymer' is well illustrated with wood-cuts in the French manner. In these wood-cuts the names of the months are given in French.

Apparently there are only two copies of this edition in existence; one is in Archbishop Marsh's Library in Dublin, and the other in the British Library. The copy in Marsh's Library originally belonged to Bishop John Stearne of

Clogher, who died in the year 1745; his book-plate is inside
the upper cover. The book is bound in contemporary
calf binding with blind-tooling on the upper and lower covers.
I am grateful to Mrs Muriel McCarthy of Marsh's for this
information.

This prayer was used at the close of the cathedral service
which marked the inauguration of one of Ireland's Presidents.
Its words were heard again at his funeral after his untimely
death a year and a half later in 1974. They matched both
occasions; personal dedication at a fresh start in a life of
service; an expression of trust made with confidence and
gratitude for the same life so soon departed.

The words were spoken and selected by President Erskine
Childers as he assumed his high office in the land he loved.
The phrases chosen from Christian worship of medieval times
clearly appealed to him. In English as well as in French each
clause has a striking simplicity and depth. Many will
remember his attractive delivery of the words, when he spoke
them on behalf of all who had gathered for that inaugural
Eucharist in St Patrick's Cathedral, Dublin on a June day in
1973. He loved to savour the language of ancient liturgy: the
Sarum prayer was a particular favourite: it was included in
the anthology *The City Without Walls* (p.29) arranged by the
President's grandmother, Margaret Cushing Osgood, first
published by Jonathan Cape in 1932. Such formal, oft-
repeated prayers are like 'other men's flowers'; they fit a
variety of human occasions and experiences. In times of joy
and in times of sorrow, the simple, direct words suit a mood
and supply a spiritual need. The wish and the petition,
couched in general terms, can set in relief the particular,
personal predicament of one who longs for God to be near as a
companion and helper. Whether the occasion be impressively
ceremonial and formally public in its solemnity, or on the
other hand deeply private and personally soul-searching, the
clauses of the ancient prayer provide a framework within
which the worshipper can move and progress spiritually.
Adaptable and lively, each phrase brings shape and order to
halting desires and muted needs.

In short, here is a prayer for everyone. The lines are easily learned by heart; they can be readily assimilated. They bring us back constantly to God with a regular repetition. God, who begins things great and small in human lives, holds the initiative throughout. The human faculties, these gifts from birth, are singled out in order that we may appreciate more explicitly to whom our life belongs and with what powers we have been endowed. The head, heart, eyes, and mouth (the list, of course, is not exhaustive) are ours, so that we may make them his, and use them for his glory. The right use of the human body is both natural and supernatural.

Dedication is the key-note of this prayer. The words inspire action. They seek to co-ordinate every part of the human frame and to relate each member and organ to the power of God and the wisdom of God. Health, joy, happiness, as well as fulfilment, will be found in a relationship which commits and binds. The words also urge renewal and restoration of a life that belongs to God, when the co-ordination has grown limp through complacency and indifference. The prayer gives balance to the life of the whole person. Our faculties are designed for such cooperation; as has been said, there are times when the head should be 'in the heart'. Spiritual progress is marked by a return to sources, by constant reference to our Creator.

Children know this prayer and often come to love it and to use it through their growing years. The words have been set to music; Walford Davies has interpreted its movement and atmosphere with a tune, irregular in rhythm, but strongly confident at the climax. It is a prayer also for busy people; its 'arrow shafts' can be directed swiftly, pointedly, with a clear aim promptly taken. At significant moments of decision and crisis, the words impress and sustain; used by candidates for confirmation, or by partners in marriage, they invite a spirit of self-giving and an attitude of strong humility. At times of sickness, or in scenes of danger and genuine fear, as well as at the close of life's journey in this world, these chapter headings for the inner life provide nourishment for the human spirit.

Each clause provides a chapter-heading for these reflections on the place of faith in the life of the Christian spent in the world about us. It is suggested that the sections may be read continuously as parts of the whole theme expressed in this 'prayer for all times'. Again, the reader may here find food for meditations, in private prayer, by reading, or re-reading at chosen intervals, such portions as match the mood of the moment or touch on a particular personal experience. This slower, or more selective, reading may also be found helpful to start a group-discussion, or to stir thoughts far deeper and more satisfying than any which these pages can hope to convey.

Chapter I

'God be in my head
And in my understanding'

The prayer starts with God. It makes a good beginning.
Indeed, the small word 'God' recurs throughout the clauses of
this song of the heart and soul. As each faculty of the
worshipper is brought into play, God is there to take the
initiative. As we recognise our failures in understanding,
looking, speaking and thinking, we are encouraged to refer
back constantly to God. He starts us on our way once more.

'God' is the small word which sums up all that is. For that
reason, this prayer in its simplicity is able to supply hope and
help in every human situation. There may well be a hundred
names for God. There are certainly countless ways of
expressing our wonder at his greatness and our love for his life,
his love, his power, his righteousness and his glory. We are
grateful for all that the small word signifies, even if we are
often baffled by the mystery of his being. We pray for a better
understanding of ourselves, although we are aware that there
is much in him which 'passes all understanding'. We are,
however, confident that 'in his light we shall see light'.

This ancient prayer which we study and seek patiently to
make our own, is full of life, at the beginning, in the middle,
and at the end. By now, after centuries of use, it is well-worn,
but assuredly not outworn. It deserves our attention. An old
favourite, it is welcomed back repeatedly by those who, after
making a sound and right start, are ready to explore the
possibilities of the whole prayer. The small words open wide
the mind and heart; they fill the whole personality with the
spirit of understanding. If 'God' is spoken of in theological
language as 'incomprehensible' because no words, no minds,
no brains can fully grasp or contain the heights of his truth

and the depths of his love, nevertheless we can grow daily in the knowledge of him and in the understanding of his will for us.

There are some famous examples from spiritual history for us to follow as we search for a better understanding of God. Prayer in the experience of the prophet Daniel was seen as an opening of the mind. This openness is an attitude for us to practise. It encourages receptiveness; it involves listening; it removes narrowness, tight tensions, proud prejudices, and dull indifference from the mind. Daniel, while in exile in far-off Babylon, 'had windows in his upper chamber open towards Jerusalem, and got down upon his knees three times a day, prayed and gave thanks to God'. With this open view, and a wide panorama stretching out before him, the prophet concentrated his gaze in one consistent direction and commented: 'When I Daniel had seen the vision, I sought to understand it'. He had made a fresh start.

It is not surprising to find difficulty in starting to pray. We learn to pray by praying. We understand more clearly the place and purpose of prayer once we have started and an opening has been made. It is a common experience in conducting a conversation or in the writing of a letter to find that there is hesitation and faltering before the opening. There are false starts to be faced and rough drafts attempted before the flow of thoughts finds an opening.

The blockage itself can have something to convey to us about the purpose of our communication. It may be a positive advantage to us not to find that the way in becomes too easy. Practised public speakers tell us that they are grateful for the involuntary twitch within that puts them on the alert. There are those who find that their difficulties at prayer become discoveries. Even distractions and hesitations can be transformed into requests and intercessions, while ease of approach and an over-confident familiarity are often strangely unfruitful.

'God is sometimes given to us as absent.' So runs a hard saying of a teacher of prayer. The paradox is salutary. Those at prayer are like the explorers who trudge through barren snows and seek to trace their way in unknown, uncharted territory. They face many disappointments as they struggle on. Only later, in retrospect, after making the hoped-for discoveries, can they see the meaning of what they were called upon to endure and the hidden fruitfulness of the strain and suffering.

The experience of Job, his impatience no less than his patience, dramatises the battle for understanding awaiting those who would grapple with the mysteries of faith and life. 'Where shall wisdom be found', he had asked, 'and where is the place of understanding?' Only after long argument and extensive searching in both likely and unlikely quarters does he discover with God's help and guidance the answer from the Almighty in these terms: 'The fear of the Lord, that is wisdom; and to depart from evil is understanding.' There are echoes of this search through suffering and testing, not only in the scriptures, but in the poetry, drama and imaginative novel-writing of the world's literature.

Isaiah's reference to the God 'who hides himself' indicates that there is nothing obvious or superficial in the spiritual vision granted to those who keep in touch with God. Such second sight is given to those who walk in faith and, as they go, make spiritual progress. Indeed it is possible to trace through the books of the Bible, both in the Old Testament and in the New, the theme of God sometimes finding people and at other times withdrawing from them, veiling himself, clouded and hidden.

The early question in the Book of Genesis, voiced by God, is a searching one: 'Where are you?' The man in question realised that he could not remain hidden from God; he admitted that fear had driven him into flight from God. A later question put to the prophet Elijah by King Ahab, 'Hast thou found me, O mine enemy?' opened the conscience of the king and gave him a new understanding of what his covetous ambition and merciless murdering looked like in the sight of God.

In the New Testament, Jesus is sometimes among people and in close touch with them, to heal and to be known; at other times he withdraws from their company. Sometimes he speaks plainly, at other times in parables. After his resurrection, he appears and then vanishes. He is with us always, to be found and to be known in different ways.

Clearly the first disciples of Jesus Christ failed on many occasions to understand their master. 'The word made flesh' expressed the meaning of his life. Discipleship involved the learning of the meaning. Gradually those who were chosen by him and were willing to follow him came to see in this human life 'the Son of the living God'. The love, the light, the truth shining in and through his life ultimately gave them an understanding of 'who he was'.

There is an attractive simplicity in the approach of Jesus to his chosen friends. He took the initiative in calling and choosing them; he wanted them to be with him, and they came to him; later they were sent out. In the phrase 'Jesus appointed twelve to be with him' there is deep insight as well as a direct method of working. The relationship was all. Prayer, too, becomes intelligible when viewed as a personal relationship of this kind. It is not a mere formality to sum up a prayer with the closing words 'through Jesus Christ our Lord'. Furthermore to extend that ending with the traditional 'who lives and reigns with the Father and the Holy Spirit, ever one God' gives our modest praise and feeblest petition its true perspective and proper worth.

'God be in my head' is a prayer which establishes a personal relationship. It makes a total claim on the one who uses it and responds to it. The mind and the heart, the eyes and the lips are all at work here. There is co-ordination in each joint fitly providing the framework and giving shape to a prayer that is lively and moving. The words prompt the offering of the whole person. For this reason our human faculties are listed with the aim of bringing them all 'into captivity to the obedience of Christ'.

The shape of this prayer aids our devotion. Just as the order and outline of the ancient Christian collects attract us by their balance, their flow and symmetry, so the rhythms of 'God be in my head . . .' increase our warmth and zest as we pray. The parallel sentences recall the atmosphere of the Hebrew psalms, where repetition signifies insistence and patent sincerity, never mere repetitiveness. The short ejaculations of each phrase in our prayer are like arrow-headed shafts piercing heaven. If they seem to over-simplify the art of prayer, then perhaps we may treat the words like the trite speech of lovers which dons a new beauty and form when set in the context of intimate conversation and personal encounter. 'God be in my head . . .' opens doors into the many-roomed house of prayer. It is a prayer that needs no book and taxes no memory. For busy people, it can be carried about as portable, spiritual luggage to calm the fuss and sort out the confusion at intervals stolen from the crowded hours of activity and rush.

This relationship with God and this dedication to a life of worshipping, loving, and believing in him is a head and heart affair. We applaud the wisdom of Solomon who prayed for 'an understanding heart'. His prayer reflects his sense of responsibility when declaring his famous wish. The application of God's wisdom to our human situation requires habitual prayer. Through the channel of prayer which continually flows, the knowledge of God increases and a fuller understanding of people and their problems is gained. The rare gift of common sense is derived from unrecognised and usually unacknowledged spiritual sources.

More than at first we realise, we learn about the nature of prayer from this desire for a right understanding. We pray to God and we search for him; we are not praying primarily for results to benefit ourselves. The actual prayer is a result and an achievement since it brings us into God's presence and helps us to 'enjoy' his love and friendship. This may seem at first to be an exalted and somewhat rarefied view of prayer, since we become so much accustomed to equating prayer with special petition.

'God be in my head' is not so much a request as a desire and a longing. We pray to be with him that he may be in us. We pray to be like-minded with God, that his thoughts may be our thoughts, impossible as this appears to be. We are right not to put slick thoughts of success in prayer to the forefront. The best result of our prayer may well be the privilege of waiting on God, of listening to him, of receiving his guidance with a mind opening up in his presence and steadily becoming more sensitive and receptive. The result to be looked for will be growth in understanding.

'Prayer, like faith, is itself the victory; the seeking is the finding; the wrestling is the blessing.' Those who have found prayer difficult and yet clearly depend upon it for their life and work give us welcome encouragement.

It may sound simple advice to urge that we should begin our prayer with God: we have the direct Christian approach with the words 'our Father' to introduce us to the trust and affection wonderfully, if undeservedly, placed in us. Yet we know that many great souls at prayer have progressed only after a prolonged struggle of mind and will. Doubts and perplexities have battled for their minds, instead of God and his wisdom.

Some have found comfort in the knowledge that this troubled mind is no new experience. They have warmed to the psalmist who, speaking for himself, has helped many another in later times to overcome spiritual difficulties. He cried 'All the day long have I been punished and chastened every morning . . . then thought I to understand this, but it was too hard for me, until I went into the sanctuary of God, then understood I the end of these men.' We do not surmise that he stopped thinking or had no further occasion to worry, but we learn that he was sufficiently humble to consider his plight with God's help and no longer to rely on his own devices as he searched for solutions to his problem.

Initiative in Prayer

Spiritual understanding is a gift. It comes by the grace of God to those who search for it. Concentrating the mind on the gifts of the Spirit we seek to become channels of God's love, joy, peace, longsuffering, gentleness, goodness, faith, meekness, temperance. So runs the well-known list which has proved fruitful in the devotional lives of many generations.

In the letters and papers of the intellectual Dietrich Bonhoeffer, we catch a glimpse of the way in which his mind worked while at prayer. When we recall that he was in prison, with his personal freedom strictly curtailed, we find his experience of the Spirit's liberating power convincing as well as astounding. A thinker with some startling ideas about the need for change in the Church, he was also practical in his stand for the righteousness and truth that were the fruit of a courageous and outspoken faith. Yet amid the danger and the daring, he found special inspiration in the longest psalm in the psalter, the 119th, which focuses the mind with a systematic thoroughness upon God's law, judgments, statutes, and commandments. In the midst of the atmosphere of revolution, and awaiting his own execution, this meditation, which is in the most favourable circumstances a formidable exercise for the mind and brain, brought him the right kind of spiritual comfort in his predicament. Needless to say, he not only fortified himself as he faced his martyrdom, but he has also brought to life for many others the words of a lengthy psalm which often appeared dreary and difficult to use in prayer.

Quotations from the psalm with the experience of this one man's prayer in mind bring a new stimulation. A human slant on a conventional, formal prayer awakens us to an appreciation of what has been well-tried and long used in the continuing tradition of the Church's offering.

'I will meditate on thy precepts' sings the psalmist 'and have respect unto thy ways.' 'Make me to understand thy precepts', he continues, 'so shall I talk of thy wondrous works.' 'I have chosen the way of truth: thy judgments have I laid before me. I have stuck unto thy testimonies, O Lord, put me not to shame.' 'Give me understanding and I shall keep the law . . . and I will walk at liberty, for I seek thy precepts . . . this is my comfort in my affliction for thy word hath quickened me. The proud have had me greatly in derision, yet have I not declined from thy law.' 'Before I was afflicted I went astray but now have I kept thy word,' 'All thy commandments are faithful: they persecute me wrongfully; help thou me.' 'Many are my persecutors and mine enemies . . . great peace have they which love thy law.'

Bonhoeffer had made a deep study of this psalm some years before his imprisonment. Apparently he had been trying for a long time to penetrate into the mystery of its verses. His academic exposition of its teaching was for him the climax of his theological life. With this background, he was given strength to endure the days leading up to his death by hanging, in Flossenbürg concentration camp 9 April 1945 when he was thirty-nine years old. His meditation on the psalm doubtless helped him to express his last thoughts with a sure confidence as he whispered to a fellow-prisoner 'This is the end, for me the beginning of life.'

The beginning of prayer is often the most difficult part of meditation. Bonhoeffer certainly did not find such devotional exercise of the mind easy; he wrote of the cost of discipleship, and his discovery that grace is always dear and never cheap gives us inspiration. Many who are physically free and outside the confines of prison feel spiritually gagged. The words do not come easily to match the yearnings of the will and the agonising of the mind and brain. The prayers of others who have triumphed in the Spirit give us hope and meaning. The simplicity, as well as the sophistication, of Dietrich Bonhoeffer's devotion was evident when, in the days before his imprisonment, his friend, Bishop George Bell of Chichester, whose understanding struck the right cord in the conversation said 'Come, Dietrich, let us start to pray by reading the Beatitudes.'

A remark like this gives us all a lead for these famous words of the Sermon on the Mount indicate where life's blessings lie. They help us to be in instant touch with the mind and will of God made known through Jesus. Those who listened found not only an understanding of God but also were given a vision of his nature in this model study of his will.

The knowledge that the humble, the mourners, the meek and the merciful, the pure, the persecuted, and the peacemakers are blessed in the eyes of God, helps all those who are dismayed and baffled by life's sufferings and injustices to understand in some way that through their struggles and experiences some blessings can be brought to a whole world in spiritual need. The word 'rejoice' later in the sermon marks the culmination of a long-term task and a costly training in the ways of service and obedience.

Intercession

Prayer for other people increases our understanding of God.

This intercession, nevertheless, is a spiritual exercise which requires sensitive treatment. We learn more deeply of God the creator when we associate our prayers with his creatures. We reach out in prayer to God with concern for others as well as for ourselves; we extend our praying with an awareness of our responsibilities as members of a family, community, neighbourhood, country and world.

In times of public distress, wars, conflicts, crises, and emergencies of all kinds, intercession comes alive with a special urgency. However, prayer for others, this moving in among others with understanding, compassion, and loving sympathy, is always timely and in place. Prayer that excludes intercession becomes quickly impoverished. Christian prayer which neglects the needs and concerns of others can hardly be called a prayer of the Church. When Christ taught his disciples to pray, he gave them a family prayer and not a merely private line of communication to God. The Lord's prayer with its plural 'Our' as its very first word intercedes in every clause for the family of God, whether world-wide or local.

Intercession is seen to be authentic and has a genuine ring when it expresses love and caring. All prayer, faithfully and sincerely offered, reflects the love of God; intercession in a particular way emphasises the radiation of that love among the human family of God.

Intercession may be prompted by events, tragic happenings, famines, earthquakes, threatenings and slaughter. Litanies took their shape and form in bad times when such evil and misfortune occurred. Yet the prayers in these circumstances are rightly for people rather than for issues, controversies, and possessions. The Christian intercessor expresses love for people, believing that persons matter more than things.

The names which figure in intercession lists should never be regarded as mere names. Even if we cannot possibly know personally many for whom we are asked to pray, we can still pray with the understanding, and not impersonally or merely formally, as we picture them with our mind and imagination as belonging to the family of God.

'Brethren, pray for us.' The words form an early Christian intercession. Emerging from a scene of suffering or persecution, names and symbols have been found scratched on stone walls, in catacombs, presenting a picture of a church, faithful even if underground, in a fellowship of love despite great loneliness and physical separation. The symbol of the cross, or a fish, beside their name signified their allegiance. The name indicated their nature and their character. Such names, human, personal, and distinct, express love and partnership. Intercession helps us to be inclusive, welcoming, generous, yet never patronising or paternalistic.

The sensitive interceder will count it a privilege to join in prayer with those who have made the request 'pray for us' in eager longing.

It is, perhaps, more realistic to pray with, rather than to pray for, others. Our chief task as intercessors is to give support and to strengthen the fellowship of prayer in which the fortunate and the less fortunate jointly share.

It has frequently been discovered that, whatever may be the effect of prayer offered for others, there is no doubt that those who remember the needy and the suffering in their prayers find their own faith enlightened and strengthened beyond their expectations. Intercessors increase in the understanding of themselves and develop generally their life of prayer. For this reason, it is important that ways of intercession should be studied so that regular and sustained prayer for people may supply consistent support and provide a whole atmosphere of spiritual cooperation. Instant prayer, without the intention of following up the first thought and wish, can hardly achieve the same measure of help. Spasmodic praying, while not to be rejected, nevertheless bears more fruit when it stimulates and enlivens a scheme or a rule of well-informed and balanced intercession.

Up-to-date information brings realism and a sense of progress to the work of intercession. While it may be right to avoid too many details or particular wishes in this kind of prayer, there is no doubt that the intercessor is helped and often inspired by the history behind the life for which he is concerned. It is not God whom we attempt to inform but rather those who will join in prayer to God. As has been memorably said: 'we do not seek to inform God but rather that he may reform us.'

Praying for others is thus seen to be a humbling activity. No special claim is made by the dedicated intercessor; virtue and piety are not professed; love and service are essential ingredients. A sense of unworthiness and inadequacy is understandably present; boldness in initiating prayer for others is tempered by the conviction that the power of this imaginative experiment in outreaching prayer comes from God.

The shape of intercession in the Church's prayers alters with the years. In recent liturgical revisions, room has been left for spontaneity within a regular framework of prayer-headings. This flexibility in the wording and scope of the intercessions produces a greater participation among the worshippers. A sense of urgency and a touch of realism make the set, familiar phrases live with a new intimacy. The prayers, offered to the heavenly Father, are appropriately brought down to earth since it is through Jesus Christ, who was made man, that we presume to pray.

Liturgically, therefore, there is at this meeting point between heaven and earth a time to praise God, with angels and archangels for company, but also an opportunity to include 'the maimed, the halt, and the blind' and to extend welcome and friendship to them after the manner of Jesus in his lifetime on earth.

Far from pitying others in their disablement and difficulty, the intercessor learns to be the more grateful for the courage shown by them in their affliction. Too often our own rude health causes our finer feelings for others to be blunted. The famous word-picture in the twenty-fifth chapter of Matthew has awakened many consciences in the world-scene of today and presents intercession in most moving practical terms. The words of judgment remind us all of our deficiencies in human understanding and the constant need for the kind of prayer that passes into service. The realisation that the suffering and the needy are those for whom Christ died stirs us to follow up our prayers with generous action. The following extract from

natic passage of the gospel puts the point, when Jesus

was hungry and you gave me no meat; I was thirsty and you gave me no drink; I was a stranger and you took me not in; naked, and you clothed me not; sick, and in prison, and you visited me not. Then shall they answer him, saying, Lord when saw we thee hungry, or thirsty, or a stranger, or naked, or sick, or in prison, and did not minister unto thee? Then shall he answer them, saying, Verily, I say unto you, inasmuch as ye did it not to one of the least of these, ye did it not to me.

The intercessor serves with faith. He learns not to be impatient for results; he realises that answers which he himself never thought of may be given in ways that pass his understanding. Yet he must not be so impassive that he loses the spirit of expectancy and hope in his praying.

Those who have sustained their prayers unfalteringly in troubled times in our country during long, unsettled years of continuing violence and much personal suffering have clearly shown a brave faith in their determination not to give up this Christian approach. If prayers for peace seemed to produce no peace, there were intercessors who persevered because the prayers had other, less obvious results. Prayer breaks down barriers of class, culture, and creed for those who find common ground in Christ for their interceding. Intercession is properly viewed as a life-work. Its results are best assessed in the language of spiritual growth, not immediately to be perceived or described.

The friends of the man afflicted with palsy, described in St Mark's gospel, certainly had faith that provided motivation and gave them the incentive to continue in their efforts to help the patient. Their deliberate resolve to lay their sick friend at the feet of Jesus for healing has become a classic example of Christian intercession. There were daunting initial difficulties; they could not make an ordinary approach; crowds intervened to block their way through. Their ingenuity in climbing to the roof and letting down the stretcher-bed when they had uncovered the roof was inspired. We learn much about the measure of their love and the depth of their compassion. The whole story of this difficult operation is coloured by the spirit in which it was handled. The results, as we know, were both physical and spiritual. No words from the four friends are quoted: the action, however, spoke loudly of the faith and love that are the fruit of prayer.

The frustration and the handicaps experienced by these friends were gloriously transformed as a result of their compassion.

The truth of what happened could be expressed in later words, written from the life of the early Church: 'knowing that tribulation worketh patience; and patience, experience; and experience, hope'. Such a pattern for those who persevere in their life of prayer has emerged in the darkest moments of depression and near-despair.

Compassion

'Compassion' is a word of considerable strength. Derived from Latin, it involves a suffering to be shared with others. There is vigour and a positive response in prayers of compassion offered for sufferers. Compassion sounds more practical than sympathy. Yet sympathy, derived from the Greek language, although it may not appear so active and even forceful in its meaning, is an important quality as well. Indicating a mood or a condition or an attitude, sympathy need not be sentimental or superficial; through sympathetic prayer, the intercessor becomes more understanding; he identifies himself more closely with the tragic circumstances and the condition of those with whom he is praying. Through sympathy, he finds an empathy; yet he never can fully claim to know what the sufferer is enduring. Sympathy, combined with compassion, fills the intercession with the love that watches and waits and the service that gives first aid and remains at the ready to make sacrifices for others. These are high standards for interceders; especially when clearly, in the words of Gregory the Great, 'it is easier to give up what you have, than to give up what you are.'

The processes of prayer are undoubtedly mysterious. This becomes abundantly evident when prayer is made for sufferers, not least when to all appearances they are innocent and undeserving. Patient prayer has upheld many in the sufferings of civil conflict. Counselling and the usual words of comfort often have failed to console; prayer must be sustained even when such devotion seems foolish and fruitless. We learn to understand that what appears in human terms to be foolish is, in fact, wise and prudent in the sight of God.

There comes to mind an incident, one of many in a period of violence with a ruthless raiding of homes and places of business. The victim in this particular case was a shop-owner, exclusively a civilian, unconnected with armed security forces or political movements. He handed over the contents of the till in response to the threatening demands of the raiders and lay on the floor with the few customers present, as ordered. Yet just as the intruders were on the point of leaving, the shop-owner was suddenly shot, receiving head, neck, and spinal injuries. Subsequently, no one could understand the reason for this final blow, unless some fear of detection caused the gunman to fire the devastating shot. For many months, this victim lay unconscious, giving almost no sign of recovery; there were only occasional flickers of recognition; only now and then did his bodily movements appear to be willed. His friends and neighbours in their sympathy and compassion surrounded him with prayer in their endeavour to help in some way. It seemed for those nearest to him in love and kinship a long and weary vigil. Yet, through the mystery and tragedy of this suffering, which ultimately ended in physical death, spiritual discoveries were strangely made by those who showed the strength and solidarity of their faith. If nothing further could be done for him by surgeon or physician to restore him to health, those who cared found new meanings in Christ's crucifixion and in the triumph of his resurrection. Two phrases came alive for one group that persevered in this particular act of intercession for more than seven months. One phrase came from the psalter with a grim poignancy: the words of Psalm 41 indicated that someone else had been called upon to face a like predicament, and as they waited patiently for the Lord their hope was that 'the Lord will deliver him in time of trouble'; they prayed 'the Lord will preserve him and keep him alive – the Lord will strengthen him on a bed of languishing.'

The second set of words that came to their rescue could hardly have brought hope and understanding with such startling emphasis had not the interceders entered into the agony of this family scene in which the wife and children and also the parents of the victim of the attack were agonising and suffering, albeit with exceptional bravery. The sentence from the epistle to the Hebrews in the New Testament made sense for the faithful 'looking unto Jesus the author and finisher of our faith; who for the joy that was set before him endured the cross, despising the shame, and is set down at the right hand of the throne of God. For consider him that endured such contradiction of sinners against himself, lest ye be wearied and faint in your minds.' This particular epistle points to Jesus who, with the Holy Spirit, was termed 'Intercessor' in the early tradition of the Church's spirituality: the Resurrection gave the assurance that 'he ever liveth to make intercession'.

The problem of pain faces us and is an experience universally felt. Such a problem can through faith and prayer be described in other terms as the mystery of suffering. The word 'mystery' is not applied lightly, but realistically. A problem certainly demands head-work from the researcher and student as a solution is sought. A mystery makes demands on the whole person, who, as it were, enters into the strange experience and permits the darkness to be wrapped round him. There may not be light at the end of the tunnel and yet progress can be made, even when in the tunnel.

The mystery of suffering becomes better understood when it is recalled that the word 'mystery' does not mean 'muddle' or 'confusion' but, on the contrary, in Christian vocabulary it signifies 'revelation' or 'the disclosing' of a truth which might be hidden or secret, but can be declared. One of the words for 'sacrament' was 'mystery'; the outward sign of an invisible quality or grace or spiritual gift has meaning for the faithful. 'The mystery of darkness' is a phrase sometimes applied to the suffering of Christ, brought about by the treachery and wickedness of those involved in the events that led to his trial and death. Significance emerged from the darkest and most dastardly of happenings. The prayer in the garden of Gethsemane has helped generations of Christians in their praying, so much so that Christ's agonising cry, 'Father, if it be possible, let this cup pass from me', has thrown light upon both the mystery and the triumph of prayer. Every Christian prayer to be properly understood must be offered on the assumption that it should be 'as God wills and not as we will'.

Suffering is incommunicable. Other people's pains can be imagined; their agonies can be compared with agonies that we ourselves may have struggled with. Yet pain is personal, and each individual has his own life to live. The suffering on the Cross, endured by Jesus, is rightly termed a mystery, and the uniqueness of his life is emphasised as we contemplate the meaning of his sacrifice. The words of the hymn are convincing:

> We may not know, we cannot tell,
> What pains he had to bear,
> But we believe it was for us,
> He hung and suffered there.

The lesser pains that human beings endure can be wonderfully alleviated with the help of medical treatment. Nevertheless, the private incommunicable ache of the proverbial tooth cannot be shared nor fully appreciated by another. The intercessor may know, as dentists professionally know, something of the discomfort and sharpness of a shooting pain, but he is right, when expressing sympathy, to acknowledge that this experience is personal and particular. Trivial as this example of a temporary or curable pain may seem to be, the understanding of its nature may help our appreciation of spiritual and mental pains at times of great sorrow and acute worry. The intercessor rejects as naive the use of prayer as protest against worry, just as the counsellor makes little headway with the superficial advice of 'not to worry'. Prayers of understanding search for the root of the anxiety. Sometimes such searching prayer reveals that the headache and worrying pain have a spiritual, rather than a physical origin.

Understanding Christian Unity

The Week of Prayer for Christian unity, organised in each year at the end of January, provides many opportunities of a deliberate kind for Christians to search for a better understanding among themselves.

These opportunities have been variously used. Where there has been the will on the part of the divided denominations to come together and confer, much common ground has been discovered. The Week, if observed in the spirit both of charity towards the separated and of penitence for failures and much self-interest, can become an exciting, even disturbing, spiritual adventure.

Needless to say, some have looked on the Week's aims and activities with caution. Unity seems far off when sincerely held convictions appear contradictory and areas of agreement are few in number.

Yet through the few who in the early days of this century persisted in prayer with no visible results to encourage them, much progress has been made in this search for a better understanding. Those early prayers were hidden from publicity. Those who pledged themselves to make intercession for unity were described as members of an 'invisible monastery'. The perseverance of the Abbé Couturier and those who followed his lead has proved fruitful indeed, although the signs of answers to their prayers were but slowly perceived. Today there is a new atmosphere of tolerance in divided Christendom and a fresh approach has been happily and courageously made. This is rightly seen as the work of the Holy Spirit stirring in the hearts of those who responded with faith, and then waited in confidence for the next steps to be taken.

The Abbé Couturier built on the foundations of others in his famous furthering of the cause of unity through organised prayer. An eighteenth-century Congregationalist, Jonathan Edwards, had started something beyond his knowing with his *An Humble Attempt to Promote Explicit Agreement and Visible Union of God's People in Extraordinary Prayer;* his movement, with this beginning, developed with a remarkable persistence. The dimensions of the problem confronting those who work for unity would indeed be declared overwhelming had not simplicity, prudence and humility characterised the efforts of those pioneers who continued steadfastly in prayer that 'all may be one' and never gave up.

The problem was described by the Abbé shortly before his death: 'There are living on the earth', he wrote, 'two milliards four hundred millions of people, one half of whom live in Asia. Nominally four hundred and twenty-two millions are Catholics, a hundred and sixty-one million are Orthodox, one hundred and fifty-two millions are Protestant, fifty millions are Anglicans. We have then a Christian world of seven hundred and eighty-five millions divided into four groups against sixteen hundred and fifteen millions of non-Christians.'

The stubborn facts provided by these statistics made this pioneer of twentieth-century prayer for unity hold firm to certain principles.

He determined that prayer should always be positive. No one should pray against another.

Prayers should be modelled on Christ's prayer, rather than in phrases framed to express a particular doctrinal standpoint. The wood-cut illustrations issued by the Abbé depicting critical moments in the life of Christ with such words from his Cross as 'Father, forgive them for they know not what they do' became famous in many countries.

Prayer should be patient, simple yet strong, penitent, and free from emotionalism or excessive sentimentality.

Such prayer should seek spiritual solutions of the tensions which easily arise among those who are loyal to their inherited faith, and yet aspire towards a new-found unity.

In one year, with the theme of 'Our Father', not only Christians but Jews, Moslems, and Hindus were brought within the scope of this prayer for unity, thus urging a fresh realism concerning the well-being of the whole world: the words on the leaflet jointly issued by the World Council of Churches with the cooperation of the Roman Catholic Church were these: 'Our Father, who hast made all men in thy likeness and lovest all whom thou hast made, suffer not our family to separate itself from Thee by building barriers of race and colour. As Thy Son, our Saviour, was born of a Hebrew mother, but rejoiced in the faith of a Syrian woman and of a Roman soldier, welcomed the Greeks who sought him, and suffered a man from Africa to carry His Cross, so teach us to regard the members of all races as fellow-heirs in the kingdom of Jesus Christ our Lord.'

Ecumenical thinking quickened its pace in the twentieth century in a world made smaller by modern means of communication and many scientific inventions. The prophets of unity came from an increasing number of denominations. Indeed the word 'ecumenism', which has the wide world of peoples in its derivation, found fresh currency after the Edinburgh missionary conference of 1910.

The overseas missionaries, whose work lay in the under-developed countries abroad, prepared the way for new approaches to be made among the Churches at home. It was easier, in fact, for the different denominations to have fellowship with one another in prayer and work when far away from home and somewhat more detached from the historically entrenched traditions which they had inherited. The sense of rivalry gave place to friendly relationships and a new understanding of the undivided Christ in a non-Christian environment. Missionaries, attempting to evangelise in Indian or African surroundings as they worked for the suffering and the depressed, were reluctant to perpetuate the controversies of European Christianity. Much that is taken for granted in our part of the world seemed irrelevant.

Archbishop William Temple, a notable precursor of the ecumenical events in our day, became the spokesman for many out and beyond the limits of Anglicanism, when he stated in language of exceptional lucidity and fine reasoning that the Christian by definition had a vocation to be comprehensive, conciliatory, and charitable in his dealings with fellow-Christians.

Temple's genius for chairmanship at inter-denominational gatherings in the 1920s and 1930s led many to adopt a new approach towards controversies that were constructive and positive in situations which had too often given rise to deadlock and cold war. It was said that he rarely brought an inter-church debate to a conclusion without a statement which included several opposing doctrinal positions in a balanced synthesis. Even if his optimism seemed unwarranted to some, his ability in promoting hopeful agreement rather than an uneasy and shallow compromise, carried considerable weight. His published readings in St John's gospel still have an important influence on those who come fresh to this method of Bible study.

In quite a different manner, the heroes of the Church struggle against Nazi philosophy and activity in the period before the Second World War, and also during the subsequent hostilities, became pioneers for unity. In the agonies of total war, practising Christians, of widely differing traditions and beliefs, drawn from Reformed, Lutheran and Roman Catholic backgrounds, were thrown together to make common cause in their struggle for the faith and for the very existence of their Churches. They discovered a new joy and exhilaration in the cooperation; they had far more in common than they could ever have imagined. The crisis of persecution and the threat of tyranny and annihilation laid bare the essentials of faith. Confessional differences and many niceties of distinction in ethos and outlook were dwarfed in the context of God's love and mercy extended to all. Those Christians, in spite of their unhappy divisions, shared their theological thinking in Bible study and life together with a new vision. When the war was over, they determined to win the peace and to develop their work for a unity, not based on fear or the demands of a national emergency but upon truth and an increased understanding of the meaning of Christian love.

It has been said of disunited Christians that, unless they meet 'face to face', they are never likely to see 'eye to eye' upon the matters which have separated them. This meeting of people, through personal contact, often brings with it surprising incidents of understanding and harmony. Even if an impasse is reached in the course of a discussion on a controversial subject, the manner in which the parties disagree without being disagreeable can become a growing point for the development of an argument or the initiation of a combined piece of Christian service unaffected by theological differences. At the very least, the meetings of persons who hold responsible positions in their Churches and are accredited representatives, remind us that the issues of deeply held beliefs and convictions cannot be put down satisfactorily on paper and left in cold print for readers at a distance to appreciate. A living dialogue must accompany an agreed statement on such matters of personal faith.

The differences within the Christian traditions concern people and what they believe. Persons, therefore, must interpret, one to the other, something of the outlook, the way of life, the ethos, which can never be merely theoretically described. Through the meetings, the conversations, and the interchange, prejudices are examined, opportunities are found for fuller fellowship, frankness of speech establishes a sense of trust, and charity is restored to the religious scene.

Shortly before the Second Vatican Council, the theme chosen for the week of prayer for unity was 'Christ, the Light of the World'. The suggested meditations helped the Christians to reach out more deliberately to those who belonged to other faiths and used the concept of 'light' in their devotions. The prayers heralded Christ as the Lord of Light and indicated that Light was reflected by Christ, and that the world was made by his Light. There was an appropriate touch of penitence in these prayers, when clearly the divisions of Christendom too often had darkened counsel, and Christians on account of their own divisions appeared to be standing in their own light. The prayers for unity prompted the questions for self-examination which asked searchingly if Christians were in fact reflecting this light. The will to seek unity, however, lets in some much needed light upon a confused world. Such measure of one-ness that the separated Christians have achieved sheds forth the light of faith out and beyond the Church's borders 'so that the world might believe'.

The unity for which we must pray is Christ's unity. For many, this means a visible unity, as God wills it; others, no less devoted to the cause of harmony and charity among Christians, do not envisage an organic unity; they regard a spiritual unity as a goal in which differences are kept intact to enrich the blend of life in Christ with variety of emphasis. Certainly, in seeking for unity, the pioneers of ecumenical action do not look for a reduction in the comprehensiveness of a faith which grips the whole person. Tempting as it may seem at times to seek agreement upon a minimum of faith and to call it unity, the patient intercessor knows that the work for unity in Christ must be thorough and far-reaching, if there is to be complete understanding and full communion.

Such variety was the experience of Geoffrey Fisher when, as archbishop of Canterbury, in the early sixties of this century he made a pilgrimage to some ancient centres of faith. He described his impressions in an account of his journeys and called the venture 'feeling his way'. It appeared to him that in the actual process of travelling he was presented with a facet of a full Christian faith and witness at each of the places where he encountered the Church. In Jerusalem, Istanbul (the old Constantinople), and Rome, three cities symbolic of the Church's history and progress, he learned something fresh and distinct about his own beliefs and the powers they possess in a world which longs for their proclamation. For him, Jerusalem signified resurrection; Istanbul, ascension, and in Rome he saw the Church serving the world and sharing in the sufferings and problems which threw light upon the significance and efficacy of Christ's Cross. He saw in this pilgrimage of unity what has been made clear by those who sustained the Week of Prayer for Unity, year by year, that such prayer is not organised for the examination of the consciences of others but to remedy our own failures in charity and understanding. This attitude must form the stuff of our genuine penitence on these occasions. As has been said: 'the more we affirm that we are in the Truth, the more we must ask God for humility'.

Unity is to be distinguished from uniformity. There can be a deadness and dullness about uniformity, while the unity which Christians seek must surely contain the warm, spiritual richness, and wide variety reflected among those early disciples who found their kinship in Christ at the beginning.

When the draft of prayers for unity was entrusted to the Corrymeela Community, some fascinating variations on the theme 'may they be one' emerged from that remarkable centre of reconciliation at Ballycastle in Ireland's north-east corner. Subjects for meditation supplied headings for the six separate days between the Sundays of the octave. Drawn up for the year 1977 these are meditations with a difference. Their wording was clearly coloured by the tragic experiences with which Corrymeela had been grimly familiar over a considerable number of years of suffering and conflict. Out of this diversity and turmoil, new facts of a faith still unplumbed, still awaiting further exploration, were brought to the surface.

The Corrymeela symbol was stamped on the cover of the prayer leaflet in that year. It indicated the meaning and the message of the week's spiritual exercises. It consisted of two crosses intertwined; one was drawn with a simple vertical line upon a horizontal: the other cross has an unfinished look, its separate shafts suggesting a cross of some solidity but not yet fitted together. Since its foundation, Corrymeela has become a community pledged to bring a new vision to the country it wished to serve. The symbol pointed to the reconciliation which follows on the readiness to repent and to forgive in a troubled and confused society.

Each of the six headings that guided the praying of that week provided a study in life's contrasts. The paradoxes of Christian behaviour were held in tension for our contemplation and study. In this way new life is given to prayer. Hope also is strengthened for those who have the courage to plunge into the conflict. The subjects continue to be fruitful, when held together in the wrestling and struggling of urgent prayer. These headings are worth recalling:

> Joy and sorrow;
> Trust and fear;
> Hope and doubt;
> Love and hate;
> Friendship and loneliness;
> Freedom and constraint.

These contrasting moods, and states of mind, will help us to sharpen our vision and to sort out the tangle of human experiences. Prayer, under these headings, produces from the criss-cross, a new pattern to display the power of God and the wisdom of God.

Many who have not been in personal touch with Ballycastle or Belfast, where Corrymeela operates, and others who have not visited Glencree's house of reconciliation in the Dublin mountains, can capture, through this kind of prayer emerging from their community life, the meaning of 'diversity in unity'. These experiments in understanding and cooperation clamour for reproduction in many other areas and neighbourhoods. Like the Week of Prayer itself, they are pilot-schemes to encourage the breaking up of fallow ground and to make some new paths towards the peace and unity 'which are agreeable to God's will'.

Praying for Peace

Prayers for peace also make demands upon our Christian understanding of the God of peace. The word itself is deceptively simple. It is on the lips of us all when there is trouble and disturbance. We ask in desperation for peace, and feel defeated when there seems to be none in sight.

We are right to search for its meaning. We can understand those who look for synonyms of peace in order to clarify their minds on the subject. We are, for example, indebted to the Old Testament scriptures for the Hebrew term 'Shalom' which gives us a deeper understanding of peace. From Israel and the Jewish tradition, we borrow this word of greeting and weave it into Christian worship. 'The peace of the Lord be always with you' is a word of worship and a greeting at a place of meeting between God and ourselves. 'Shalom' is also heard in the lands of the Bible when stranger meets stranger, and pilgrim hails pilgrim.

This welcoming introduction of one to another is like a pass-word which opens up many a conversation and bridges the gaps in our social life.

There is something more positive in the peace of Shalom than in the peace which is too narrowly defined as absence of war.

'Shalom' speaks to us of the wholeness of life, the healing

qualities of fellowship, and the inspiration that comes from faith in God to add to life a fullness and a hope, and to transform it from mere existence or survival into a purposeful and satisfying human experience. 'Shalom' is active inasmuch as it prompts movement and meeting among people. Its meaning is specially forceful and productive when it is operative in situations where there have been stubborn fixities of attitudes which have become outworn and prejudiced. Where too there is a dull or deadly uniformity that has stunted growth in the community and has arrested normal development, the peace of 'Shalom' can revive a spirit of service and active concern for the welfare of people everywhere.

Wherever there is a meeting of minds and personalities, wherever there is to be found a bridging of gaps between generations, across creeds, over the divide of social, political, and communal separations, peace proves to be creative and healing. Such bridging is not designed to bring dullness to debate or to eliminate the sparkle from argument and remove honesty from personally held opinions. Peace is not equated with mental lethargy or the craving for a monotonous sameness in views and characteristics. As a sign of greeting and meeting, it enriches personal life, creates harmony and opens up opportunities for the development of personal gifts and talents.

Those who pray for the peace which is found in the doing of God's will, as God's creatures, give an important lead in their role of peace-makers. Their prayer reveals that they are ready to share their lives; they are prepared also to operate in the spirit of a peace based on truth and justice, filled with love and hope, wherever an opportunity for peace-making is found in their local scene. This sort of peace can be created on the doorstep of each person's home, and in the immediate neighbourhood. Its productivity may well be unlimited. Such small beginnings, in a word or gesture, lead to undiscovered ends. Its results are unknown, probably unexpected, and certainly incalculable.

We pray to God, in the old phrase, as 'the author of peace,

and lover of concord'. We remind ourselves that peace is a gift bestowed, not a feeling from within. The gift of peace, when received by us, leads to that other kind of peace named 'concord' in which we have an important responsibility. Concord is the fruit of the peace of God which grows through personal relationships in human scenes of home, family, community, and country, if the response to God's gift is faithful and consistent.

Such peace has a binding power; it heals sores and wounds, and binds up what has been broken. Peace calms disturbances. Within the mind, and outside in the world, it is a force and a movement. It has been compared by a prophet of old with a river which streams through barren and unresponsive territory to make deserts and wildernesses fertile with a welcome growth. Peace is development. Peaceful trade between countries holds out a promise of life to the hungry, as they starve, and to the despairing in their agony of want.

Yet there is nothing simplistic in the concept of Christian peace. If peace has binding force, it is itself bound. Love undergirds it, and holds it together. Charity, in the fullest Christian sense, is 'the very bond of peace and of all virtues', to quote the words of a prayer that has become a classic. Peace is found in a person: the Christian knows him 'who is our peace'.

Peace is, therefore, more than a state of mind, or a condition of life, or an inner calm. It is an agent of love. Christ with his peace, which he gives to us, is recognised as a reconciler, as reconciliation itself. 'He has made of both, one.' He drew others with the ties of love. He gave people his particular peace which was called, in turn, forgiveness, healing, and friendship. He gives these things still.

There is a discipline in the search for peace which we dare not ignore if we wish to make a find. Peace is more than a word, a catch-cry; it is possible to shout for 'peace, peace,' in selfish exasperation and to have none of it, when the shouting is over. Peace is a way of life; as we know, it 'comes dropping slow'.

The hand stretched out in the midst of Christian worship, when the peace or the *pax* invites trust and love and fellowship, commits the heart. The old custom of passing on the 'peace' with a hand-clasp for our fellow-worshipper beside us has had a revival. In South India, with the spirit of reconciliation among many Christian groups alive and active, white hands joining with coloured hands at the parish communion impressively extend the scope of peace. Hands of every colour, culture or creed on days of prayer work in harmony to remove those disturbers of the peace, familiar to us in the shape of enmity, malice, prejudice, apathy, pride, racism, bigotry, and crude sectarianism. Peace is a binding force, even when the clasped hands are loosed again.

Peace joins the extremes and gathers together the frayed threads of good intentions, better feelings, and half-formed wishes that have blurred the pattern and spoiled the effect. 'The end of art is peace', the poet interprets for our better understanding.

The embrace of peace was counterfeit when Judas treacherously kissed his Master. His misuse of the sign of peace was black betrayal. We are bound by the discipline of the true peace; this is a costly discipline and cannot be cheaply dispensed. The peace 'that passes understanding' follows upon true repentance and a personal undertaking to be in love and charity with our neighbours; such are the simple, but straightforward, prerequisities to the receiving of him who is our peace.

One practical experiment in peace-making made a lasting impression when I visited the staff and students of 'a school for all nations' on Canada's western coast. Away from particular scenes of conflict and misunderstanding, this stay at an international centre of education proved a tonic for many who too readily find their spirits drooping in the face of current events in today's world. Not every nation, of course, was represented by the young members nominated by their own countries to assemble in this college to pursue their studies in an unusual setting, on the edge of the Pacific ocean, and to meet each other for the first time. The thirty-five countries involved, however, provided a substantial sample of varied points of view, characteristics of culture and traditions of religion. The burning issues of Middle East, of West and East, of Third World with second and first world, added to the problems of countries internally divided, were represented by these unofficial and youthful ambassadors.

The school is situated among gigantic fir-trees, their sturdy trunks standing at solemn and straight attention to protect the college buildings, their tree-tops reaching for the stars. Within these woods, the sloping paths link together class-rooms, assembly hall and residential buildings; library, restaurant, recreation rooms and administrative offices fill the interstices of the network made by these woodland tracks. The way down towards the harbour and the inlet from the sea invites the visitor to the landing-stage where the boats crowd at anchor. Here is a point of departure for those who after a two-year stay of study and world-experience will move on, outward bound, with a new look on life and an increased understanding of its complexities.

The remoteness of the place and the sense of its inaccessibility provide opportunities for the members of all these nations to cast a detached eye back upon their own home and native land. They also have a rare opportunity of sharing in relaxed conditions the cultures and aspirations of the mingled company. Here community is made, and the seeds of peace are sown. There is an openness among all, and a readiness to serve and to give assistance where the untrained or the disabled are in need or difficulty. A service of worship lingers in the memory. The chaplain from Eastern Asia had the formidable task of bridging traditions of worship, and including Christian and non-Christian elements in this expression of fellowship. Some words were clearly common to all in the gathering: peace and understanding were the subject of prayer; likewise praise and thanksgiving for their life of fellowship together and for the link which bound their nations and countries in harmony won the participation of all. If the Christians broke bread in communion, with eucharistic thanksgiving at the heart of their worship, many who were not Christian and were in no position to participate nevertheless received in other ways the message of peace and reconciliation which the liturgy was seen to convey.

Moving also was the witnessing of contributions to the

understanding of peace, when transmitted in the idiom of other religions, often without words and without interpretation, yet unmistakably communicated through the atmosphere of peace prevailing and the stance and bearing of those present in a fellowship of silence.

When all was over, it became clear that religion was not intended for divisiveness. Differences were clearly there, and yet they commanded respect even when full acceptance was not possible. The languages in use were many in that school, and the classes small. Teachers and the taught were strangely interchangeable. Each one had something distinctive to contribute to the whole. Staff and students had much to learn from one another. There was an easy flow of minds, both the young and the more mature. Ireland had representation there; those from other countries were eager to learn about the island's life and history. Experiences from all the countries, both searing and healing, were shared in the search for answers to the common human problems and the predictable questions; many answers came through the life rather than through the languages. Prayer, as well as thought and argument, played an intelligible and significant part in this place of education, sited away from it all, on the margin of a great deep.

Chapter II

'God be in mine eyes
And in my looking'

God gives us vision. We pray to him that he may open our eyes that we may behold 'the wondrous things' of his law.

If God starts us in our meditating, he helps us to see what is invisible. 'O world invisible we view thee.' Francis Thompson expresses the thought for us, introduces us to that kind of world, and invites us to share in the vision God has given him. 'O world intangible, we touch thee,' he continues, 'O world unknowable, we know thee; / Inapprehensible, we clutch thee.'

We find God in unlikely places, but also in conventional settings, if we are sensitive. He makes us stare with surprise. He catches us unawares. 'Open wide; open wide; it is God.' The words of that simple prayer are fitly found in the porch of a church; the worshipper entering has his eyes opened.

Francis Thompson again expressed their experience:

> The angels keep their ancient places,
> Turn but a stone and start a wing.
> 'Tis ye, 'tis your estrangéd faces
> That miss the many-splendoured thing.

We sometimes find this to be a genuine reaction where prayer has come to be made in a hallowed spot, teeming with history, where worship has been valid. In the company of angels and archangels, we see with a difference and our spiritual awareness is awakened.

We can look, as Dame Julian of Norwich looked, at a hazel-nut small and round. Holding it in the hand we can say with her, 'Behold, all that is.' We are not surprised that her writings have recently stirred fresh interest, and her kind of prayer, with its vision of the Creator and his creation, has had a revival.

The artist of the Book of Kells, concentrating on the spirals drawn with the finest delicacy, counted it worth his while to toil faithfully over the most minute details which the normal viewer will scarcely see. Even if the naked eye passes over the intricacies, unnoticing, the artist was certainly convinced that God saw his work. Others also, who work with similar dedication, recognise the worth of a masterpiece, in stone or on canvas, completed not for profit, nor even for instruction, but in response to the inspiration of the artist's vision.

If God sees such expressions of beauty and order, then it is fitting to pray that God may be in our looking. Such a prayer gives insight and opens windows for us upon what has been puzzling and perplexing. We pray that God may direct our eyes and give that way of seeing which perceives not only the surface but the art, the dignity, the meaning of what has been fashioned.

The looking, with God's help and in his company, brings illumination. When we hold ourselves still in his presence, we see more clearly than we could have imagined. Here is no straining of sight, no gazing upon crystals; this stillness is experienced as relaxation. Our eyes at first may rest upon what seems ordinary and dull, to discover later that there was more here than met the eye. In this way, an inspired work delivers up its secrets to the trained observer.

The eyes, resting on a phrase as on a picture, behold new meaning and contemplate fresh truth.

St Augustine, in his *City of God* written at the time of the sacking of the 'eternal' city of Rome, peered into the life beyond the grave, and prophesied that at death 'we shall see'. Perhaps also, when we shall know as we are known, we shall concentrate our gaze and discover much that now is veiled.

'If thine eye be single, thy whole body shall be full of light,' Jesus said. This single eye, of which he spoke, provides the concentration, the sincerity, and the enlightenment for those who would follow in his way. We suffer too often from double-vision and even double-think; we find ourselves unable to focus our sight upon essentials; we feel 'sure of nothing' without God's certainties.

The thought of Psalm 139, expressed in the language of most beautiful poetry, provides the spiritual answer to the common problems of many a questioner about religion. 'Lord, thou hast searched me out and known me,' the psalm begins, 'thou knowest my down-sitting and mine uprising; thou understandest my thoughts long before. Thou art about my path and about my bed and spiest out all my ways.' There is so much to see, we find it hard to be selective in our looking. We long to have the gift of the kind of sight which relates the small things, which we see and observe, to the whole picture 'of all that is'. We pray for a true perspective. The psalmist takes up the point and proceeds to express our feelings; 'such knowledge is too wonderful and excellent for me, I cannot attain unto it.'

It is God who does the looking. Now, we see in a mirror, 'darkly'. It is all most enigmatic. The reflection comes to our notice. We reflect, as we behold his glory, that, subsequently, not now, but then, we shall see him face to face.

We recall for a moment that thin line of 'seeking and finding and hiding' which runs through the scriptures. There is both a glorious revealing and a mysterious reserve to be found within the Bible's narrative. Moses' face shone with borrowed light when he descended from the mountain after his vision; he had talked with the Lord, face to face; yet, it became clear that man was not to see the face of God, but only the 'back parts' (Exodus 33:23, A.V.). On another occasion, the chosen three with Jesus on the mount of Transfiguration were given a glimpse of glory, which in the plain below had quite another kind of appearance. It was certainly not obvious that the way of the cross was a way of light. This truth had to dawn later.

The old Irish hymn:

> It were my soul's desire
> To see the face of God

takes us to the heart of prayer and to the core of faith. This vision of God will be granted to the clear-eyed, the pure in heart, who will see him as he is. It involves looking in the right direction, facing up to him with penitence and courage.

There is also much mystery in this kind of looking. When we learn that in our life of faith, a mystery has been shown to us concerning, for example, the life of resurrection, we realise that the mysterious secret becomes a revealed truth. God is in our looking to help us to uncover the hiddenness of something obscure and baffling. The contemplation of the mystery of the resurrection is a spiritual experience. 'Behold, I show you a mystery,' St Paul wrote in memorable words recalled at the graveside, 'we shall not all sleep but we shall all be changed; in a moment, in the twinkling of an eye, at the last trump.'

The famous prayer associated with the name of the Curé d'Ars helps our looking. When the old man, at his devotions for long hours in the vastness of the empty church, was asked about the content of his praying, he replied with the simplicity that prompts the direct approach to God: 'He looks at me and I just look at him.'

The eyes of the portraits of Christ, painted in some of the early medieval manuscripts of the gospels, penetrate the reader and appear to be designed to fascinate. We might paraphrase this experience of the riveting eyes: 'he looks through us, as we look at him.'

The Coventry Cathedral tapestry with its gigantic design depicting the Christ in majesty, dominates in the sanctuary. The eyes search out the viewers and cut them down to size; they also challenge and compel. There is mercy in the majesty; there is also the straight look of the fair and just judge.

If God is to be in our looking, then we must ask that we may be enabled to see people and things with his eyes, his standards of judgment and his immense perspective.

'In thy light we shall see light', sang the psalmist. In God's light we examine our prejudices and take that honest look at ourselves with a brave humility.

There are times when we can pray best with our eyes open. We should not always take it for granted that we are right to shut out the world of sights and sounds, when we converse with God. Indeed, we increase our confidence and our faith, if, with open eyes, we know where to look, and how to look.

Whether at prayer or not, we need grace at times to sustain a steady look, without flinching, without shiftiness.

Prayer can be offered in the lifting up of the eyes to behold the thing that is good. The tree, the mountain, the blue sky, the fleecy cloud, the wide sea delight the eye, fascinate the gaze and win from us a spiritual response.

Some churches with windows of plain glass have a devotional atmosphere of their own, on account of the contact which the eyes of the worshippers find with the natural beauty of the local surroundings outside.

There is a chapel, on the edge of the sea of Galilee, greatly beloved by pilgrims and tourists, who enjoy the spiritual hospitality of this building. Its east window of clear glass opens up a glorious view of the water out to the hills on the other side of the lake. The sparkle, as the sun catches the surface, the flaming colour of the flowering shrubs on the water's edge, the shadows, and the shafts of light bring to the worshippers' gaze an awareness of wonder. As we look, wide-eyed, we praise. We think of the *Benedicite* in a new light: 'O all ye works of the Lord, bless ye the Lord; praise him and magnify him for ever.'

Visitors to Glengariff on the inlet of Bantry Bay, County Cork, have a similar experience to tell. The memorial window that admits a view of the famous island-studded harbour, a gem of natural beauty and rich foliage, contains one thought to inspire those inside the church. The inscription, 'The heavens declare the glory of God' sums up the view. The transparent window above these words and the glimpse of God's creation beyond add their own testimony. The worshipper is encouraged to see and to praise. The plain window frames the colourful picture.

The prayer 'God be in mine eyes' is far from being a redundant request. We may be able to see thoroughly well, but often we fail to perceive. We look, yet we are less ready to observe. While we may at times notice something in the picture or the view that others have passed by, there is much which we miss.

Again, we are inclined to see, with a marked self-interest, the things 'we want to see'. We are skilled in ignoring the unsightly. We see issues and problems in blinkers that isolate our vision. We find our vision narrowed, surrounded by influences that blur our vision and distort our view. We may cast a critical eye over much that comes in sight; we forget that, in making our own judgments, we ourselves are being continually judged by God. Our criticisms reveal much about ourselves and our way of looking at life; we are woefully transparent and easily give ourselves away. God shows us up; other people also show us up. The prayer 'God be in mine eyes' should make us thankful, even for the painful and humiliating experience of being shown ourselves, as we really are.

Our prayers become more honest when we remove the veil, the mask, the façade and all that covers up. We have obvious sins and weaknesses that many of those who live near us and work with us have already recognised. We have also invisible sins; we sin against the light. We leave things out of our life: such omissions, often culpable, are evident to God. They are to be discovered in that grey area of personal life where there is an insensitivity and a lack of responsibility. Our awareness of need loses its zest. We become preoccupied with our own concerns and forget that 'no man is an island'.

In the parable of the good Samaritan, the priest saw the victim of the robbery but passed by on the other side; the levite reacted slightly differently, insofar as he approached the place of the disaster and 'came and looked on' the traveller, lying half-dead, but then passed by, without taking action. The Samaritan also saw, and we might reasonably suppose that God was 'in his looking', for he responded compassionately and gave the practical first aid that has made his good deed proverbial. The spirit of alert and altruistic service shown by the Samaritan has brought out this reflection: the Samaritan did not say to himself when he came upon the scene 'if I cross the road, what will happen to me'? His reaction was quite the opposite: 'if I do not cross the road, what will happen to him?' This was his way of looking at human being in trouble and suffering. That decision and action challenge us to go and do likewise, with our eyes opened.

We might ask if we ourselves are sufficiently imaginative in our looking. Looking involves relating. We need the help of prayer and counsel in perceiving causes and effects in the events around us; the interaction of personalities claims our attention, and tests our powers of observation. As we look, we should also appreciate where there are difficulties in the solution of which we can cooperate. In disputes and controversies, we are right to look at every side of the issues, and to appraise the points of view which differ from our own.

Some of our looking is frankly dull and dim. There is also the humbling fact that we look at objects mostly from our own end, as C. S. Lewis used to say. We confess that our looking is also often for our own ends. A predatory look enters our eyes as they light up with an understandably gratified and probably selfish sparkle before something particularly tempting and appetising. A sour and begrudging look is equally to be overcome and rejected, lest we kill the joy of life and cast a green eye of jealousy upon the happiness of others. Looks can kill in more ways than one.

If God is in our looking, we pray for grace to sustain, in our regard for others, the loving, caring and forgiving, associated with our knowledge of God, given to us in the life of Jesus Christ.

We are right to remember the evidences of Christ's looking, not least when our own eyes lack lustre. We allow our eyes to assume the bored look in our depression and self-centredness, or the glazed look that betrays our carelessness or callousness, or the far-away look of the uncommitted and the uninterested.

With Christ conditions become quite different. The gospels help us in our looking. Jesus' relationship with Peter, for example, for all his faults was summed up in a look at a criticial moment of betrayal. 'The Lord turned and looked upon Peter,' we read, after the cock was heard to crow. 'The eye of the Lord lighted his darkness.' was the comment of John Donne upon that moment of conscience. The look of love conveyed a spiritual message, too deep for words, too deep even for tears. Looks can save, through this sort of communication; even if, at other times, they can torment. We pray that we may exercise 'the good eye', and drive off 'the evil eye'.

'Lift up your eyes.' This is a call to worship to match the ancient 'Sursum corda,' 'Lift up your hearts.' Raise sights. Widen horizons. See next steps. Look round corners.

Looking back has its dangers. Yet in retrospect, we remember with thanksgiving God's goodness, unrecognised at an earlier stage. We give thanks as we remember his forgiveness, his patience, and his guidance.

We look to the rock whence we were hewn, with similar gratitude. We owe much to our tradition and heritage; they claim our regard. We dare not stay in the past, however, imprisoned and even blinded by an excessive, disproportionate longing for what is over. We value hindsight as an aid for the undertaking of responsibilities in the present.

The prophets, in Old Testament days, interpreted past events with vision and wisdom. Hindsight increased their foresight. Not always as seers, more often in their proclamation, judgments, and forthtelling, did they fulfil their public role in the country. Even when days were dark, and there was no open vision, their unswerving trust in God enabled them to read the signs of the times. Their faith gave them their insight.

Exploring

There are numerous ways of praying. Songs, words, silences and also sights provide us with a framework for our life of companionship with God.

Sacraments, those outward and visible signs, all help the sustaining of that life, and remind us that ultimately we depend on invisible means of support, such as the gifts of faith, hope, and love, which God bestows.

Prayer is not bound by any particular pattern, mould, or convention. Where the Spirit of the Lord is, there is liberty. Work has been defined as prayer in some circles – especially when we perceive in the work, when accomplished, something of the vocation, dedication, and beauty which the finished product expresses. Prayer is drained of its power and significance if it does not in some way or other express love. The wood-carver sets about his work in the right spirit as he looks at the rough branch, now separated from the tree, studies its graining, recognises its texture, and running his fingers over it, loves it.

So we think at times of prayer as a very human act of life and love in terms of exploration. Prayer is stimulated when we look upon it as an adventure, an exploring of the things of the spirit in many areas of ordinary experience.

Thus, prayer moves out from the framework of liturgy, away from set forms and phrases, to be free ranging, spontaneous, extempore. Into the open, prayer stretches with advantage; into the unknown it leads us to create new opportunities – possibly into a wilderness, where prayer has not hitherto been tried. Here there are innumerable openings, and virtually no limits. Vision is required for these ventures. 'Where there is no vision, the people perish.'

Prayer becomes fluent when all sorts of insights stir random ideas and eccentric notions within us. Exploration can begin with the familiar phrases of Christian worship; from there, we are led on and out into the perplexities and anxieties that may seem to distract us and frustrate us as we pray; yet in many cases they sharpen our vision and help us not to lose our way. Thus we trace new paths of spiritual progress on our pilgrimage. St Catherine of Siena spoke of the importance of training young children to be observant, to notice the details of life, and to keep a sharp look-out in their early years; she went on to say that in later life the things seen in childhood, which stirred the imagination and filled life with fantasy, were no longer necessary as props and guides for the vision of God and his love granted to mature hearts and minds at prayer.

The explorer in the uncertain ground of doubts and disappointments discovers that worries are transformed into deeper concerns. In the dark night of the soul's journey, new light shines and faith grows stronger after the testing and the blinding.

Through exploratory prayer, spiritual deserts for all their barrenness and waste-lands become irrigated and are made fertile. Such prayer searches for the uncertainties and seeks to shed light on life's ambiguities and inconsistencies. 'Light looked down and beheld darkness; / Thither will I go, said Light.' The poet was interpreting the meaning of Christ's birth, when the Word was made flesh, and we beheld his glory.

There is no element of protest or confrontation in this process of exploring, listening, waiting patiently for a glimpse or a gleam of an answer or a clue. We make time on this journey for our eyes to become accustomed to the mist and the gloom. With an awareness of God's presence, we learn to live with the obscurities. Abraham's example of obedience and faithfulness still inspires the traveller. He went out, not knowing whither he was going. He kept his eyes open; he looked for a city without foundations, 'without walls', whose builder and maker was God. He had enough insight to keep moving on. He was strangely conscious of the general direction in which he should go.

Searching

One of the earliest service-books used in the worship of the Irish Church refers to the festival of the Epiphany as 'the star'. The *stella* of the Stowe missal helps us to find new meaning in our response to the light that shone in a very dark world, when the Christ-child was born.

The search undertaken by the wise men from the east is a continuing search. The more we study the world and its creatures, the greater seems to be the demand for further research. The mysteries of creation seem the more mysterious to those in the know, who have already made some remarkable discoveries.

Teilhard de Chardin confessed that his scientific studies increased his sense of wonder. He never allowed himself to treat creation with an over-familiarity. He used to declare that the oftener he looked at nature and its workings, the more mysterious and the more exciting these things became. His was an unfinished task, he cheerfully admitted.

The wise men – whether they were kings or philosophers or scientists, or all three we do not know – have much to tell us in our foolishness as we grope for the truth and seek for the answers to our problems.

'They all were looking for a king.' So the carol expresses it. From their experience, we have learned that we are not left alone without guidance, to search for a way through. God searches us out and knows us; he provides the starting point and gives us the lead. The journey made by these travellers from a far country was a pilgrimage of faith, made in the dark, for a religious purpose. There was a gleam of light, a star to guide them on a venture which showed the world where the true values lay.

The look which discerned the star in the heavens was doubtless a steadfast look, for travelling was not an easy pursuit. It was a bad time of year for a journey. The sequel to the discovery of the child they had looked for was by no means easy or pleasant. The doubts and difficulties of the travellers who had made their journey were followed by critical and jealous questionings and the opposition of another king. The desert journey may have had its hazards, but the turbulence of the market-place, with the publicity given by the lookers-on, added further tests to their faith and vindicated their quest for the truth.

The wise men opened their treasures and they presented their gifts. These gifts were, of course, symbolic. The infant king who received them could scarcely be enriched by such offerings. The gold, and the rest, however, indicated that those who made these presents were prepared to give themselves. Their worship and their eye-witnessing were of great significance.

Later on, Christ's words, 'seek and you shall find', brought great encouragement to his hearers. When they began to look, they discovered themselves, and found a new place in their world. They could not seek God, had not God already found them: yet when the search began, they found that they had more scope for their talents and gifts.

Vision

Vision and value were on one occasion the themes for

worship and meditation at a university graduation ceremony. The students' course of study had been completed and their life-work, following the obtaining of their professional qualifications, was about to begin. Those who received their awards felt they had earned them; they were now looking ahead. They prayed for vision, as Christians, like the students in monastic days prayed centuries ago. They linked sight with hope in their prayer in those earlier days when they looked out from the headlands of the island's coast-line across the sea. It was a long view, if a lonely one. 'Be thou my vision,' they would sing in the words of the hymn which has retained its popularity to this day.

The scholars of old sought not merely knowledge, as they studied their subject. They hoped to know themselves a little more clearly in the fellowship of learning and the school of discipline.

In every age, the rivalries of life's competitiveness sharpen human judgment and disclose our limitations. To be, rather than to know, is seen to be the right goal of the heart's desire.

Yet the knowledge, in part, of things studied on the prescribed course is a necessary preliminary, while life develops and experience teaches.

Those who know in part long to see into the dark of the unexplored future and to find the meaning of the life entrusted to them for true enjoyment.

The vision of this future comes with a single eye, rather than with that double sight which lacks the power to focus, and takes us off course. The vision of God granted to those of pure intent, of honest approach, of prophetic insight is the only satisfying achievment of life here – and beyond.

Such a vision shines through training, through the acquisition of skills, the sifting of facts, and the evaluation of data. The inventor sees through his experiments to new discoveries. The researcher handles his material with an eye to the interpretation of it, and an assessment of its worth. There is partial vision in every pursuit undertaken by student and scholar; yet, 'he who sees through everything, sees nothing' the epigram reminds us.

In the search for truth, the guidance of the Holy Spirit

points the way. The famous seven gifts, listed in the Bible, meet the needs of those who have studied and are now qualified and ready to serve in the world. They were right to pray not only for wisdom but also for understanding; not only for knowledge but also for the inspiration and counselling that make hard facts living and active. They were right also to pray for reverence in the handling of their subject, lest pride and self-assurance should blind their vision and stunt the growth of their understanding. Godliness and good learning go well together.

The end of the course for the student marks the beginning of a career. The qualification indicates that the grade has been made, but it opens our eyes to the gaps in our knowledge. The question 'Why?' and 'To what purpose has this course been undertaken?' can only be answered in terms of sharing and serving in the world about us. The vision for the expert, the specialist, and the professional must ultimately be a vision of love, if it is to be fully satisfying. The worth of the work, at human, social, communal, or family level, is enlightened and enriched by the love of God, which passes understanding, and excels all ambitions, desires, hopes and longings in human hearts.

Spiritual Research

Christian prayer is a credible subject of research. All of us who look to the practice of prayer in our everyday living as a source of inspiration are indebted to those who have passed on the fruits of their spiritual research. Whether we realise this or not, prayers composed by others have come to our lips in time of need. The solitary specialist in the field of spirituality has given public service beyond his knowing.

Helen Waddell has written sensitively and delightfully about the desert fathers who in their day were specialists in the spiritual life. She understands that others might well ask what has been the value of this eccentric life, spent away from it all, in the sands of North Africa. She suggests that we might as well ask the purpose behind a polar expedition and the dangers encountered by the trained team of explorers who tramped through the snows day after day in apparently fruitless endeavour.

She compares also the marathon spiritual exercises of the monks in the early centuries of Christianity with the zeal of the racing motorist who trains and perseveres on the spacious track to improve his speed, which already has far exceeded any pace that could possibly be allowed to an ordinary motorist on a public highway.

Increased knowledge and heightened efficiency are gained for the ordinary citizen as a result of such closer looks at creation's resources. Prayer is the better understood after explorers have trained themselves to tramp over barren snows and to wander into the wilderness in the interests of finding out more in the field of the spirit. In this way, the knowledge of God is increased.

Transfiguration

Our prayers cannot be offered with such intensity – nor perhaps at the same speed! Yet the research undertaken by men and women of remarkable dedication and vision, in spite of some acknowledged eccentricity, has enriched Christian life to our great advantage.

We benefit in particular in our life of prayer from the example of Jesus. We see from the evidence of the gospels the part that prayer played in what appears to be a short ministry, filled with movement and activity. The wilderness, the mountain top, the place apart, the experience in the garden of Gethsemane all provide scenes from which we can learn about this faculty, this skill, and, some would add, this art.

In these settings, we see Jesus more clearly. The mount of Transfiguration provides a particular opportunity for a clearer vision of him.

Those who are fortunate enough to go on a pilgrimage can find in the expedition another form of research.

Today there is much to see at the summit of Mount Tabor, the traditional scene of the vision granted to Peter, James and John, whose eyes were remarkably opened to the radiance and glory of their master's personality on a memorable occasion.

Mount Tabor stands out conspicuously in Galilee country. Its slopes rise abruptly from the high road below. The path to the mountain-top twists and coils in more than twenty hair-pin bends. The summit is impressive, not so much for its height, but more for the striking view that can be gained from this vantage point.

A church of gleaming stone and colourful frescoes has been built there, dedicated to the transfigured Lord. Here he had been seen in glistering robes. His appearance was described as glorious. His companions saw his glory. The building provides a moving reminder of the vision granted to those who had entered the cloud.

From this height, a magnificent view allows the eye to see the mountains of Gilboa, the land of Naphthali and other places associated with the people of the promised land, which find mention in the Old Testament.

It is difficult for the pilgrim not to reflect upon the significance of the climb made to that conspicuous spot by Jesus and his disciples. On this occasion clearly the disciples held in their hearts and imaginations strong associations of ideas. Moses had been on a mountain where he was granted a vision of a special kind. He had also been commissioned to undertake far-reaching responsibilities for the people in the plain below, whose leader he was.

Elijah, the prophet, had received an unusual vision when alone and apart with God. His withdrawal enabled him to have ears to hear a still, small voice and to find its sound more eloquent than the crashing noise of an earthquake, the howling of the wind, or the terrifying crackle of a raging fire.

The companions of Jesus, in a comparable way, saw more clearly who their master was, as a result of this gloriously blinding experience on the mount. The words of a teacher could not make as deep and lasting an impression. This moment of mystery, worship, and ecstasy had an outstanding vividness. This was a day to remember, a sight to look back upon, a timeless and revealing experience.

The vision was given to the faithful, the specially chosen even if unlettered disciples in order that they might perceive and know what they would be called upon to do and suffer.

The top of the mountain was certainly not out of this world. The height did not symbolise any kind of escapism. What happened up there shed new light upon the toil and trouble awaiting them on their descent to the foot of the slopes. The later encounter with the epileptic child in need of treatment and cure brought another kind of reality to the ascent and its sequel. The transfigured Lord was, after all, down to earth. He was willing and equipped to deal with human problems.

We find that there are two visions given to us in this Transfiguration scene. The vision of glory and the vision of grace confront us. We are grateful for this kind of double vision. The grace of God through healing, reconciling, peace-making and wholeness in our lives is the seed of the glory. The vision on the mount enables us to see a vision of love and responsibility, challenging us to be concerned about what is sordid, disordered, and repulsive in the life around us, and to take action.

An important message to be received from the contemplation of such an other-worldly event as the Transfiguration concerns our future. The incident is a reminder of the purpose and end-product of quite trivial actions, and small but timely opportunities of service that are presented to us. Too many of us find no interest and little meaning in what we are called upon to do. Too often no vision of a future, of work completed, of a satisfying aim, comes easily in sight. 'When you're dead, you're dead,' some say, and display their unwillingness to probe further into this mystery. The vision of Christ transformed, glorified and renewed, is granted as a corrective to such pessimism and bewilderment. The sight of 'Jesus only' shed a brighter light for the disciples on their immediate future and on the life to come. Those who saw this shining light were poised between one world and another. They knew that they were not there by accident.

There was a very different atmosphere on another hill-side when the friends of Jesus were in his company. From the slopes of the Mount of Olives, Jesus beheld the city of Jerusalem and wept over it. The sight of those tears was not to be lightly forgotten. The weeping inspired some to erect a modern church on the supposed site. It marks a moment of emotion and truth. The dedication *Dominus flevit* (Jesus wept), is a rare reminder of the Lord's passion and inward agony. The building is a visual aid towards the understanding of inexpressible grief. The architect designed the church in the shape of a tear-drop. A wide window of plain glass looks out upon the towers of the city below. It provides a framework for the famous sky-line, glowing somewhat luridly at the time of the sun's setting. The city, thus sighted, shows its towers and historic landmarks. Within its walls there is much that the archaeologist is still revealing. Much remains hidden; much, too requires interpretation and explanation in terms of faith and prophecy. Jesus' tears can only be properly understood in the light of a past history of chequered events, the story of a people and a nation.

Inside the 'tear-drop' church, a hen with her clutch of chickens gathered close is depicted in artistic colourfulness on the face of the sanctuary's altar. The words of anxious concern and loving care spoken by Jesus, as he looked down at the city, are movingly recalled by this farmyard scene of nurture and protection. 'If thou hadst known,' he said, addressing the city, 'even thou in this thy day, the things which belong unto thy peace, but now they are hid from thine eyes'. Such was the prophecy about the city's impending destruction. In another recorded address to the city, we read the words of Jesus, 'How often would I have gathered thy children together, even as a hen gathereth her chickens under her wings, and ye would not.'

Those who make the journey to the great city of Jerusalem, as pilgrims rather than mere sightseers, discover more from their contemplation of this view than any guide-book can express. They can picture, as if it had been re-enacted, the encounter with the world undertaken by Jesus. In that setting, with its background of religious history, what is hidden and indeed invisible is perceived by those who stand where he stood.

There are visitors to these sites who have found their faith strengthened, and even kindled, as they looked on these scenes. A pilgrimage can soon become a journey of discoveries. Those who enter into the spirit of the history associated with these places find the unexpected, and learn in a new way that faith is a gift, often experienced before it can be explained.

The tears of compassion on the hill above the city sprang from a deep longing for the people concentrated there. There was love at the heart of this agonising and spiritual suffering. If only the inhabitants had known the things that belonged to their peace, those in the city might have had a very different kind of life. This is the tale of many cities.

In every scene, there is much that escapes the eye of the beholder: looking is not enough. Surveys and statistics present us with the measure of the problem. There must follow the interpretation and the reading of the figures and facts, if a proper estimate is to be found. Faith and foresight, linked with the looking, teach us the secrets of things that are not seen.

Seeing and Believing

Seeing, in Christian writing, and particularly in the New Testament, is often linked with believing. Not that seeing is believing; but believing is kindled and finds fresh sparkle when there are signs and evidences to encourage faith.

It was probably less difficult to talk about death, for example, after the news of Christ's resurrection had spread among the community of the faithful. Eye-witnesses had pooled their experience. They repeated and recorded what they had seen and heard.

After the astonishing event of the first Easter, death had taken on a different character. Death now meant for the faithful, who saw and believed, a lasting companionship with the risen Master. The word could be looked at with a steadier gaze. Death lost its chill and gloom. To die was to go where the Son of God had gone.

In spite of this new view of life – and death – it is still not easy for Christians to speak about that one of life's certainties which is physical death. Whether they have courage to cast a cold eye or a confident eye, on death as well as life, there will always be a sense of mystery to accompany the experience of those who have reverence for life. They know that there is more to be considered than the physical death which meets the eye.

Resurrection is a cause for joy: it draws the sting from death. Looking back at the event of resurrection, the first believers were joyful and thankful. The accounts of what happened are complex: the descriptions provided by eye-witnesses of the risen Lord varied. For that reason, their reports are convincing and have the ring of truth. Their looking has been personal, selective, and immediate.

We note the varied human reactions to the central fact of a faith, now nearly two thousand years old. The witnesses in St Mark's gospel leave us amazed. The description of the terror and the trembling makes us correspondingly humble. The silences are eloquent, the fears are most telling. We are grateful for the sense of wonder conveyed to the reader by this staccato, somewhat stunned, reporting. If we find ourselves able with more confidence to talk naturally about death, we become aware that at the same time our new-found freedom of speech must give recognition to the shock and mystery of each one's death, however much the event has been expected, however much we have prepared ourselves for it. There is still the feeling of 'being diminished' lingering in our thoughts, subtly expressing our appreciation of a life that has been part of our lives, until this change came.

The future is to the fore in St Matthew's Easter narrative. He links what has taken place with the earlier teaching which prophesied what would happen. Galilee was the place of training for the disciples when they were called to follow; they went back to Galilee, to become apostles with a world-wide mission. Wherever they went, they themselves would be visual aids for the proclaiming to the world of what they had seen. Their faith was full of resurrection hope and Easter joy. After that first day of the week, everything was new, but history continued.

St Luke's gospel characteristically shows his predictable feeling for people, as he writes. He links the promise of resurrection to the lives of those who argue and question. His account of what took place proves a help to others who have not seen. He brings this new dimension of hope and spiritual victory into their lives with his emphasis on prayer and worship. He is the writer who describes the supper party in the village, when Christ was made known to those who were at the meal when bread was broken. Luke's final words for his New Testament gospel remind us that the Christian gospel never ends. He reports the continuous process of 'praising God,' in this world and the next.

St John's gospel has light and life for its theme from the very first chapter. His presentation of the good news is filled with radiance and glory. At every point of human existence, signs of God's glory are to be seen. In scenes of hunger, sickness, blindness and, as in the Lazarus incident, death itself, Christ's light shines. 'Death and glory' is the consistent message that enables us to sense the invisible in every visible and tangible experience. We are not disappointed when we turn to St John's record for signs of life and shafts of light where much seems dead and dark in our world.

The Eagle Eye

St John's gospel was the choice recently made by the churches in Ireland for joint Bible study. Roman Catholics, with Presbyterians, Methodists, and members of the Church of Ireland followed up the suggestion made at the inter-church conference in Ballymascanlon during the seventies. Others from the Society of Friends, Moravians, Salvation Army, Non-Subscribing Presbyterians, and Lutherans also participated in this shared study of the Scriptures. All had something to contribute; all had something to learn.

The reading, discussing, and thinking together opened the eyes and minds of those who from their differing backgrounds of belief and worship revealed what they had personally discovered from this Fourth Gospel. All, as a result, benefited from the combined operation. Many insights increased the understanding of those who had come together to learn and to be enlightened.

St John's gospel has been called 'the spiritual gospel'. It was found specially suitable for joint study since the meaning of the events in the life of Jesus is declared with particular emphasis in the clear arrangement of this gospel's structure.

The eagle has for long been the symbol of St John's gospel; perhaps because, as has been said, 'the eagle alone of all living creatures can look straight into the sun and not be dazzled'. So writes that well-known expounder of New Testament writings, William Barclay. He continues on this theme: 'John has the most penetrating gaze of all the New Testament writers into the eternal mysteries and eternal truths and the very mind of God. Many people find themselves closer to God and to Jesus Christ in John than in any other book in the world.'

The essentials of the faith are here expressed in very simple words, many of them in ordinary use and of one syllable only. Yet when the writer discourses on light as well as on life and love, we find ourselves plunging deep into the mysteries of these apparent simplicities. For that reason, discussion, meditation, reflection, and the bending of many minds upon such words become a rewarding exercise for those who are ready to give time to make spiritual discoveries.

St John's purpose in shaping his gospel in his special style and form is declared towards the end of his final chapter: 'so that you may believe that Jesus is the Christ, the Son of God, and that believing this you may have life through his name'.

His narrative is shaped by events. The birth, death, and resurrection of Jesus all have a deep significance. The signs which structure the gospel disclose the meaning of what happened: it is a book of signs. 'In the beginning was the Word' he opens, and sustains the record right to the end, expounding that Word's meaning. Christmas, in the language of John, is the Word-made-flesh; the meaning, not the place of the birth, is the significant point on which he lays his emphasis. The wonderful works of Jesus are signs; the healing of the blind and the paralytic are signs of sight and life.

Events are selected for description and linked with the festivals and seasons so that new meaning is given to the familiar features of temple worship and the traditional ceremonies of the Old Testament. The lamb, the shepherd, the vine, the manna in the desert, and the Temple itself, all illustrate something deeply significant, yet radiantly glorious, about the Christ.

'That was the true Light, which lighteth every man that cometh into the world.' Phrases such as this abound in the book chosen for study among the churches in a time of trouble and conflict. The contrasts, drawn by John, of light and darkness, truth and lies, knowledge and ignorance, show all of us who are ready to think on these things, as we read and discuss, that there is a more excellent way of life available which cannot be destroyed by violence. It is not without significance that lecterns in churches, from which the scriptures are read, are designed with the form of an eagle whose wings support the covers of the book, while an eagle eye invites our attentive gaze, as we listen and look.

Seeing and Perceiving

The word 'see' recurs with great frequency in the gospels. There are several distinct ways of expressing the use of the eyes. Beholding a view or gazing upon a scene is a very different experience from looking on a person, perceiving, as eye meets eye, something of the other's character or mood: response of intelligence or sympathy from the look that lights up the facial expression can be seen with an immediate sensitivity by some, but will be missed by others less perceptive.

Jesus taught much to the physically healthy, who were strong in limb and sound in health, by his sensitive approach to the disabled, handicapped by loss of sight or paralysis of body. The perceptiveness of those, who could not see with their eyes or hear with their ears, proclaimed a very special sort of spiritual good news. God was evidently in their looking, even when eyes and ears were impaired. The mind's eye of the blind could have sharper vision than the fully sighted who, while able to see everything around, perceived little, and were strangely unobservant. Jesus found in his encounter with the blind Bartimaeus as he begged by the wayside a remarkable response. One whose sight had failed recognised and acknowledged the master. He was given sight: the healing was attributed to the beggar's faith. His spiritual insight had made him whole. There was more perception here than could be found in the crowds looking on. The beggar made a more discerning response than those critics of Jesus who seemed to be blinded by their prejudices.

'Have you believed because you have seen me?' asked Jesus after the resurrection. 'Blessed are those who have not seen and yet believe.'

'We have seen the Lord,' said the disciples, all together with the exception of doubting Thomas. 'Unless I see in his hands the print of the nails . . . I will not believe,' rejoined Thomas. Yet the same doubter was soon to say 'My Lord and my God,' and we realise that God was in his eyes and in his looking just as much as he had been in the eyes of the other disciples.

A later question was put to the first Christians: 'Why stand gazing up into heaven?' Asked at the scene of our Lord's ascension, there was clearly both a rebuke and a challenge in the question. To gaze and gaze on God may be ultimately the highest activity and the most deeply longed-for experience of all, but the devoted followers of their Master were not called, in spite of all temptation, to stand rooted to the spot where they had glimpsed the heavenly vision. They must not carry their heads in the clouds, as though held in some ecstatic trance, searching wistfully for the unobtainable.

From Sight to Faith

A vision, a vivid spiritual experience, can be strangely exhausting. The moments which follow the fade-out of something inexpressibly moving become depressingly flat. The keen eyes of the companions, who had watched every movement of him who was with them, and was now taken out of their sight, assumed the dull, glazed stare of the astonished and the perplexed. They lacked the shining of the eager, forward look of the hopeful and the expectant. It was apparently but a momentary experience for these bystanders, temporarily stunned. Their stare unfroze; they knew that there was work waiting for them.

The withdrawal of the Christians after the Ascension was

silent and logical. Without fuss or manifesto, Jesus had left the little company standing. The time for withdrawal had come; the beloved disciples perceived that they should use that moment of vision as a signal for action. His parting did not mark a conclusion: their lives, temporarily brought to a stand-still, as of men thunder-struck, suffered no arrested development. Their Lord was not absenting himself: he was advancing. With royal progress he went before them and intended subsequently to draw them after him. When he had ascended, he was more powerfully present with them, 'closer is He than breathing, and nearer than hands and feet'.

The Ascension is not a subject for the geographer. We are not concerned with a place to which he has gone. It is idle to gaze up into heaven in the hope of piercing the blue haze above with a telescopic sweep of the eye. We are rather concerned with what he is now doing. We ask about function, not locality. The account of the Ascension is noticeably brief, but keenly suggestive. The miraculous, aerobatic element in the event fades into the background before the significant and culminating truth that Christ is set free to be available for the world. He is no longer locally present at the Hill of Bethany, but is universally present in the hearts of the responding faithful. He has gone up; 'up' refers not to elevation, but rather to eminence of power and superiority of rule. We look up to the ascended Lord; we look back on Calvary where he was crucified for us. He is above in the sense in which a leader gives directions from above; he is on high, for life with him is of a higher order with loftier standards. We look to Jesus 'the author and finisher of our faith, who for the joy that was set before him endured the Cross, despising the shame'. His very exaltation inspires us to come down from the clouds, and to extend our sympathies to the world in which he left a few to be his witnesses and his agents.

The Dark is Light Enough

We find ourselves praying in the dark sometimes with nothing to look at. The darkness of doubt can extinguish the desire to pray. There is nothing there, we say: nothing to be seen: not a gleam.

Others have told us that 'the darkness is dazzling'. Mary O'Hara spoke of 'a dark cloud guiding her' in a time of exceptional difficulty. W. E. Gladstone wrote a hymn with the opening line 'O lead my blindness by the hand.' Many have thanked God for the darkness; it has much to teach; it helps us to doubt our doubts, to turn again to faith after a break, to pray in a new way, with a fresh start, a break away from a dull continuity.

The darkness of suffering, bereavement, injustice, descends on us at times to terrify and leave us chilled. Some do not find these things dark. Words of comfort such as 'Fear not, only believe' come to their rescue. That word 'only' well deserves a second look. We perceive the darkness of evil because we care and we love; some have a passion for finding a way literally and spiritually through dark nights to a new dawn. The rule of the community of Taizé helps us here: 'renouncing henceforth to look back, and joyful with an infinite thankfulness, never to be afraid to precede the dawn to praise and chant Christ your Lord'. When we recall that the founder of this Calvinist community, Roger Schutz, with his companions, emerged from the confusion of a war-torn France in the forties of this century with that kind of vision and resolute spirit, we too give thanks for the dawn they welcomed through the darkness.

Some people simply do not see the unpleasantnesses that others are called upon to endure. We find ourselves too often looking the other way when there is a tragedy in which we might find ourselves getting uncomfortably involved. Or, again, we simply have not looked in their direction: there are times when unawareness becomes irresponsibility. In violent days, news of woundings, killings, robberies, and intimidations is announced so frequently that our minds become unmoved and our eyes fail to observe and take notice, and compassion fades away. Jesus looked at life with an outstanding clarity: God was in his eyes. He saw Nathanael, for example, before Nathanael saw him or came within range. He also saw into, and perhaps saw through Nathanael, and perceived that there was no guile in him. Not even when he asked the somewhat sceptical question: 'Can any good come out of Nazareth?'

In all this kind of looking, this observation of invisible qualities, near at hand or at a distance, we take note of the place of vision and insight in our Lord's life. They were symptoms of something wider: 'You will see greater things than these, you will see heaven opened,' he had said.

Look to the end – *respice finem*. This is a timely reminder for us when at prayer. Look through the wounds to the healing. Look through the darkness of sin to the forgiveness and reconciliation, to the loving relationship restored, and often strengthened.

Look to the end, to a fulfilment, as we offer prayers for peace in a long and continuing struggle. 'The end of your faith', to quote the first epistle of Peter 'is the salvation of your souls.'

Chapter III

'God be in my mouth and in my speaking'

A preacher finds this a ready prayer as he mounts the pulpit. He adds his concern about the words he has prepared to the prayer we have just studied, 'God be in my eyes and in my looking'. The speaker communicates with the tongue, but also with his eyes. His aim is to establish a relationship with his listeners. He speaks not into the air, but to people. They have a share in the communication through their attention and response. In this way the message comes across from speaker to audience.

A sermon, by definition, 'joins' preacher with people. There is the element of conversation in this kind of utterance, even if the people remain silent. Their response can be clearly sensed by the speaker, who becomes aware of the differences between rapt attention and hostile resistance as the words are spoken and the discourse continues.

The teacher, the preacher, the story-teller and the ordinary conversationalist, the parliamentarian and the actor on the theatre's stage, are all aware of their listeners in their varied efforts to make their point and convey their meaning. Such communication comes alive and effective when inspiration quickens the utterance. The person speaking has an individual style. His prayer that God should be in his mouth and in his speaking is appropriate when his desire to communicate himself, as well as the words which serve as a medium, becomes evident. The sincerity, the ring of truth, the honesty of expression, the choice of words, the gift of illustration, the touch of humour, and the warmth of conviction may all be in the speaking. If the faith and love of God are present also, then the answering of the prayer no less than the asking becomes all-important.

The Language of Prayer

Divided Christians in recent years have united to study and discuss the language of prayer. Those who have long been accustomed to go their separate ways as worshippers, have discovered that they share a common problem. Together as Christians, they have opened up discussion on the whole question of speaking to God. They have all derived considerable benefit from the combined examination of the language of prayer.

'How should prayer be best expressed?' they have asked each other. 'In what idiom, in what style, with what words?'

'When you pray, say Father.' The words of Jesus used in his instruction of his disciples serve as a familiar headline for the consideration of prayer as a conversation, with God as a partner in the dialogue.

The word 'Abba' used by Jesus was a popular name, an intimate, friendly mode of address. It would have been understood by young and old, alike by the educated and the illiterate. It had as an opening greeting a human and loving ring. So personal was its sound, when uttered, that it established a relationship difficult to describe, but unmistakable when experienced.

The affectionate 'Abba' introduced a blend of receiving and giving, of respect and warm familiarity, of love and trust, of belonging and identifying. Dwelling on the word, the speaker finds relationship.

From an understanding of this little, child-like word 'Abba' as a means of communication, we are able to appreciate more vividly that same word's overtones, its love and its trustfulness.

The Lord's Prayer has an atmosphere which is both traditional and contemporary. Translated into scores of different languages, it has echoes in its phrases and clauses which were familiar long before the days of Jesus and his disciples. The wholeness, however, the balance and the comprehensiveness of this prayer have given it, as presented in the gospels, a special authenticity. Jesus gave a model for use down the centuries. Traditional in its wording, it is certainly alive. The song of this prayer from West Indian lips with the haunting refrain 'hallowed be thy Name' assures us of that. There have been countless imitators of this modern setting that has turned the prayer into a 'song to remember'.

Those who studied the language of worship in some depth found that they were reluctant to abandon the traditional style of speech which they had inherited and which had become part of their culture. They were, however, determined to eliminate what seemed to them to be archaic and obsolete. As they reviewed a problem which all in different ways shared, they were anxious that reality should be found in the words they used. They recognised that a contemporary idiom requires for its enrichment the special words of faith and experience that have emerged from some of the spiritual struggles of Christian history. The champions of the faith gave a special accent to the words that matched their witness and their sufferings. 'Father, forgive', scratched on the walls of the bombed cathedral in Coventry, were words that have helped new life to emerge from the fire and blasting. Borrowed from the words on the Cross, they flank a cross of charred beams and crooked nails to indicate in a very special way a deep love and a new relationship with God.

Clearly, the Lord's prayer, without its biblical echoes and the 'period' words which have enriched our vocabulary, would find the modern usages of our current language, in which we seek to present its petitions, both flat and fleeting.

A modern prayer need not abandon 'in-words' which the Church, as a family, has used for generations. A word from the past, whether it be sacral or technical, gives bone and body to a longing and a desire pouring out from the heart.

Perhaps a poet, rather than a drafting commission, is needed for such balancing of what should be fixed in a prayer and what should be free in its expression. The formal combined with the flexible will preserve truth and introduce a note of joy and delight. Sincerity and a sparkle of human feeling make prayer attractive as well as serious. The formal and the familiar confirm the old, reliable relationships between ourselves and God; the current idiom and the free speech of devotion match the deeply felt needs of today and provide a response to the spiritual hunger and thirst of our time.

Counselling

A neglected gift of the Spirit is the spirit of counsel. Where counselling is practised in prayer or in conversation a new awareness of answers to prayer is often found. When hearts are low and hopes run out, a word exchanged with another can open the way for a word with God. We may seem to have provided our own answers to the problems that faced us, but we realise that the sharing of a worry is a lifting of its weight, to our great relief. The opportunity of speaking about what had been unspeakable helps us to look at ourselves and our troubles in a new light.

Those who took 'sweet counsel together' and 'walked as friends' found a common bond in the God who had given them a faith to share. There was little joy in hoarding the faith possessively in churlish, even surly isolation. 'The whole counsel of God' is a generous and large-hearted description of the truth, wisdom, justice, and love that all of us need.

A time for counselling, when sought, becomes spiritually rewarding. The tradition that prompts such soul-searching in the season of Lent is worth reviving. Counsellor and counselled find common benefit in the atmosphere of quiet and reflection associated with the spiritual preparation for entering into the passion of Christ.

God, speaking through the counselling, makes more of the guidance than any one adviser or specialist in the field of human problems can rightly measure. There is room in such encounters for the Spirit to move. The Spirit also uses the weak and perplexed to bring fresh courage and insight to the other members of society who have dropped out and are in loneliness. Renewal of life follows an awareness of short-comings and limitations.

The listener contributes to the findings of such counselling.

His response may be silent, yet receptive. The fellowship of such silence has power to heal the open sores of the human spirit. In any interchange through dialogue or in group discussion, what is not said can be as important as many a speech of exhortation or flow of professional advice. Censure will rarely be productive; sympathy likewise is usually not enough. What is done through counselling can gain new significance from the company which hears the human story of trouble or need and sets it in true perspective.

The worship in which the Christian shares the fellowship of the community or congregation, has within itself the power to bring the worshipper to a deeper understanding and knowledge of himself and his problems. The words of Scripture become on occasions uncannily relevant; the music of the choir, the participation of the people, and the silences, combine to teach us the mystery of ourselves and to point us to the way in which God is guiding us.

One simple piece of advice may help our predicament and bring release. Elijah the prophet was directed, he knew not why, to sit under a juniper tree, and wait. His obedience and readiness to listen and be guided prepared him for the next step.

The spirit of counselling is not usually as instant or abrupt in operation; it provides a continuing resource on which we can draw, confidently and patiently. The answers to questions that spring from dryness and doubt in the spiritual life come, not snappily, but more often with the unnoticed growth of seeds, which sprout and surprise us. Long-term solutions are unpopular in a world of instant news and pressing haste. It is in watching and listening that we give the spirit of counsel its chance. Then we venture to speak, we seek to keep God in the conversation. St Patrick described his prayers in such terms, and sensed that the words he used were not his, but rather that God was speaking in him.

A Famous Dialogue

The walk to the village of Emmaus on the outskirts of the city of Jerusalem after the resurrection of Jesus is a remarkable example of communication. St Luke's gospel carries an account of the incident, expressed in his artistic, literary style with a choice of words well worthy of study.

The two, who were walking together on the road that led from the city, were talking about all that had happened recently, the trial and the crucifixion of Jesus, and the tragic events connected with his death.

They were sharing their experiences. 'Communing' is the word which translates this conversing with one another. The evidence of what happened becomes stronger when two points of view are available; two witnesses, rather than one only, help to fill in the picture and to establish the facts about the event. Two witnesses meant that there could be an interchange of words to express feelings and experiences. They were conversing about what they had heard and seen, and in their speaking they had obviously shown emotion and their personal reaction. For when Jesus joined them as they talked together, he was 'in their speaking' and asked why they were sad; he also questioned them about their conversation, and walked along with them.

'Walking' was a word that indicated belief as well as behaviour in biblical language. The faithful were encouraged to walk in the spirit. Noah walked with God and in doing so revealed his loyalties and convictions. This walk on the Emmaus road was not only a scene of dialogue, but a means of developing a theme through conversation. 'Those who speak to one another, love,' is an African proverb which sees in conversations which have not broken off, or collapsed, a relationship of friendliness and sympathy. When speech proves impossible, hostility and a cooling of relationships result.

Walking companions speak now from one side of the road and then from the other. Thus question and answer, proposal and counter-proposal, observation and corroboration cause the subject of the discussion to be fully examined from several points of view; its implications for those engaged in the conversation are more deeply understood.

This village of Emmaus (of which 'the exact location is unknown') became lastingly famous for the talk on the road and the subsequent vision of Jesus when, sharing the evening meal, he was seen in the breaking of the bread. The talk of the road is enshrined in one of 'the world's' immortal short stories. St Luke in his account, by his accurate use of words, gives us eye-witness reporting instead of idle gossip.

Christian talk could with advantage model itself upon the pattern of the conversations on the Emmaus road. They were talks about happenings, not just talks about talks. They were talks with a difference, since the topic of their talk was present with them, searching them, questioning them, as they went along. The person in question was the risen Lord.

They argued and they reasoned with one another, and so through the dialogue they came to a balanced view of the matter under discussion. Cross-talk becomes productive; facts are tested in a cross-examination. Interpretation of the obscure elements and the inevitable rumours was required. The stranger appeared to hold the key to the problems. The talk ceased to be despairing and perplexing when Jesus arrived. 'He expounded unto them in all the scriptures the things concerning himself . . . thus it behoved Christ to suffer and to rise from the dead the third day.' With Jesus present, the unknown became well-known.

The good news of the gospel should circulate rather than stay enclosed in a fixed formula, locked in permanent print, in terms, theological and professional, valid for a period and yet prone to be outworn and deadened as life proceeds. The impact of the good news is made when people receive and listen: they have an opportunity to ask questions and to reveal their own reactions. What they glean from the good news depends much on their own perceptiveness or the awareness of their own needs. So Christian truths come alive in creative conversation, in good travelling company, at the tea-table – or the breakfast table – or even over dinner, in house-groups or over the fireside after a television discussion – and in many kinds of fellowships. With a free interchange of thoughts and views, memories are jogged. St Luke applied the word 'joint research' to this piece of team-work undertaken by Cleopas and his companion, when the stranger joined them.

After the walk, the talk continued in new tones and at

greater length. Luke, who was both historian and evangelist, records with masterly understatement that the others 'were told what things were done in the way'. They could not, in fact, stop talking of an experience of a life-time. Another evangelist, in the fourth gospel, doubted if all the books in the world (even if they should all be written) could contain all the records of the many other things that Jesus did. This sort of talk spread round the world and, in doing so, it provided the material for teaching and preaching the Christian faith.

Before we Speak

The Greeks had a delicate way of indicating that speech is not improved by wordiness. Their expression for silence was 'good speech'. Ironical perhaps, and even sceptical as this sounds, they had a point.

If, in our prayers, we ask God to be in our speaking, we must also accept the fact that, in order to hear him speak, we are wise at times to listen, without uttering a word: 'There is a time to keep silence and a time to speak.'

There are also occasions when we defeat our own ends. What we are shouts so loudly that those present cannot hear what we say. Our words, even if not obliterated, are reduced in weight and worth on account of the weakness of our character and credibility. Too great a fluency obscures the point of our words, if we neglect the pauses. The selection of words makes demands upon our patience and intelligence. We appreciate the feelings of the psalm-singer who 'kept silence, yea even from good words' when in the presence of God, whose word was with judgment and authority.

Silence, therefore, is good communication at times. Silence has been declared golden. The Christian at worship has much to learn from holding still in the Lord, and cultivating receptiveness. Places where silence is traditionally observed help us to keep our mouths shut, and to hear the answers to our requests, without any interrupting from us or any obtrusion of our own opinions and suggestions.

A quiet corner in a noisy world has an eloquence in its atmosphere.

> Let all mortal flesh keep silence,
> And in fear and trembling stand.

These words have their context in the sanctuary where speech is halted and the outward and visible sign of a sacrament tells a fuller story than any words can express.

The lines attributed to the first queen Elizabeth put the point:

> Christ was the Word that spake it;
> He took the Bread and brake it;
> And what that word doth make it;
> I do believe, and take it.

The silences amid the singing and the prayers in a country church are precious. They charge the scene with the presence and the grandeur of God. In a place apart, surrounded by the noises of nature, the bees humming, the water lapping, we become aware of a silence that is almost tangible. The stillness increases our sense of wonder. It stimulates a reverence for life and a deeper love for all creation. It puts us humbly in our place.

Silence, however, is not only found through a selfish withdrawal from the traffic of life. There is a corporate silence to be discovered in worship with others. Body language and spiritual language, as we stand or kneel or sit, in silent prayer or quiet listening, bring to the words, which we may use later on, a new sincerity and a greater modesty. Such silence, if it becomes part of our communication with God, is freed from artificiality and self-consciousness. The deliberateness of those unhurried, unruffled, wordless, soundless moments of worship banishes from the intervals and the pauses any sense of unease and mental discomfort. There are those who display their nervousness by excessive talking. The tongues which run away, with the speed of verbosity, are disciplined and controlled through the practice of silence.

Silence, at times, can overwhelm. Some fear those intervals

which punctuate a life of activity. They dare not relax or let go. They do not trust their powers of enduring aloneness in the midst of much ado. Nor is it surprising that when a group or a congregation is exhorted to observe a time of silence, after the preliminary process of settling down in quietness, a deeper, second silence descends movingly on all present.

It is not surprising that the climax of the hymn quoted above, which bids all mortal flesh keep silence, should be a quiet, confident word of praise. 'Alleluia' is sung and repeated when the presence of God is experienced.

This word of adoration, 'alleluia', 'praise the Lord', is gentle, grateful, peaceful. It does not disturb the silence; it echoes God's voice. It could be said that God was in our vocal prayer. It is as if the godward side of us was responding to the manward side of God. Max Thurian, of the Taizé community, called this quiet burst of praise, so happy and so humble, 'the joy of heaven on earth'.

Just as the long 'rest' in the music of a famous symphony eloquently conveys the composer's message before the final burst of sound, so silence in worship can be a deeply significant act of worship. The silence which comes over the audience at the end of the recital before the applause, provides a further illustration of this experience.

In the Apocalypse, we read that when the Lamb opened the seventh seal, there was silence in Heaven about the space of half an hour. During that space, a great multitude waited in recollection and alert expectancy for a vision which was given to those whose hearts were ready to receive it.

Jesus was accustomed to go away alone into a desert place – not for ease or escape, but to see more clearly the scope of the work for which he had been sent into the world. Apart and surrounded by mountains and silent rocks, he faced the spiritual issues involved in his life's work of ministry to people, to crowds and to individuals. Thus, before the practice of his preaching and speaking began, the principles were thought out and spiritually assimilated. So far from finding emptiness in the desert, he wrestled and agonised in spiritual combat with the opposition of the tempter. He was given what to say by the Holy Spirit in such a time of trial. Our withdrawal to a place where prayer is taught and practised in the silent fellowship of believers adds a maturity to the understanding and vision of life's purpose. The relaxation in a place of retreat, after experiences of strain and stress, alters the mood and makes a refreshing break before the usual duties of daily life call once more. Thoughts, habits, and emotions assume a new shape after research-work in the things of God has been attempted. Such withdrawal is a valuable prelude to any verbal expression of the fruits of our inner meditation. The silence of the quiet place banishes the trivial and the malicious from the mind and heart; God speaks in such a setting. To listen to him, when there is little to distract, is the purpose of the withdrawal.

C. S. Lewis, a master of words and a prolific writer, has revealed in one of his letters how much an opportunity of silence and recreative rest meant to him in his year's programme of teaching and counselling. His business, as university professor and teacher, was largely with words and his genius for explaining spiritual truths with clarity and brilliant style has brought many to accept the Christian faith with joy and strong conviction. In a letter to a friend, Lewis writes of his delight in the Irish countryside, the land of his birth. He picks out for special mention the landscape of County Donegal, the quiet place and beautiful surroundings which provided him not merely with rest, but with inspiration for further speaking and writing after his holiday had passed. Those, who are familiar with the scenery which pleased the author of the widely read *Mere Christianity* and other writings on Christian faith and life, can picture him relaxed among that country's 'delectable mountains', as he described them. Lewis said they had a radiance which made them appear through the morning mists to possess three times their actual height. Even on the moist and duller days, he writes with enthusiasm of the lovely shafts of light which break through the blanket of cloud, in a countryside where the brightness after the rain gleams with a proverbial suddenness.

'Be still' and 'know' sang the psalmist. The words of this spiritual song have been interpreted not in terms of grinding to a halt in the midst of our activities; and dropping everything with a suggestion of irresponsibility. This stillness which we seek is not laziness or idle numbness. 'Be still' is more likely to mean 'have leisure and know,' give some time to God and his word. It is not only restful but actually invigorating to make time for the presence of God when time has been relentlessly demanding. To have time, and to spare some hours, for thinking and reading and companionship will bring renewal of ideas and a more ready speech as we try to put into words our prayers and praises.

Good Words

Bad language is notorious for the forceful impact it makes upon listeners, and the shock it administers. Good language seems to attract less attention, and, in certain human situations, to be less effective.

For all that, the good language of Christianity has often proved powerful, moving, and sometimes revolutionary in unexpected quarters. It is an exciting experience when we find that the word of God is still 'quick and powerful and sharper than any two-edged sword, piercing even to the dividing asunder of soul and spirit, and of the joints and marrow, and is a discerner of the thoughts and intents of the heart.'

A study of the recorded words of Christ helps us to discern why his language was self-evidently good. To begin with, he spoke with authority. Secondly, his smallest words, his throw-away sentences, and even his silences quite clearly emerged from a life of complete integrity. Furthermore, he spoke to the needs of the moment, applied his words to heal those whom he met, whose sicknesses and sins he fully understood: he answered with point and power when people put requests to him perhaps out of ignorance or, in some instances, out of malice and deception.

The authority that Jesus exercised in his speaking led him out of the comparative obscurity of Nazareth into the limelight of his public ministry of preaching and teaching, and brought him subsequently to his death. He spoke against evil and all that was devilish. He challenged the conflicting authorities that opposed him. He came out strongly to condemn the bad language of hypocrisy and proud arrogance, wherever he heard it.

It became evident to those who followed him with loyalty and love that his words were genuine and uncomfortably true; others held that his speech was blasphemous. He knew what people were thinking, and was competent to describe with accuracy and penetration the characters and personalities of those with whom he came in touch.

His commands and rebukes had power to bring control to a confused situation. He calmed the storms with a word of peace. At his trial, when he answered 'never a word' to his accusers, he was movingly eloquent.

We search for his very own words in the records, the *ipsissima verba* of his ministry in the world. We treasure the fragments of his speech which have survived; his words of healing and his words from the cross, as he hung there and suffered, have an authentic goodness. We study the gospel writings which report with the help of eye-witnesses and ear-witnesses the essential points of his speeches and sermons. We know that what was seen and heard has been declared to us with a faithfulness upon which we can rely. 'This is the record, that God has given us eternal life, and this life is in his Son.' Small wonder that he himself was called the Word, 'the meaning of it all'.

His words sprang from the faith that he imparted to others. Every word and sentence issued from his life of perfect union with God, the Father. Good words became even better, when on his lips.

Christ was not to any great extent a coiner of new words. The words he used were not, in the ordinary sense, original. Yet when he spoke the language of religion, his listeners were introduced to a human and most personal conversation with a difference. They had heard nothing like it before. The persons in question, whether disabled or sick or sinful, to whom Christ's words were addressed, revealed through their healing experiences the power of his speech. Words from Christ's lips, which sounded quite ordinary, became extraordinary and had a richer meaning. Words like 'love', 'grace' and 'faith' have gained a special fullness of meaning since they took their place in the Christian vocabulary. They have become technical terms with a great potential in Christian life. Each of these monosyllables is properly related to God's life and cannot adequately be appreciated as merely human language. 'Love' for example has obedience in its heart, and perhaps a cross also; 'grace' has a beauty given by the Spirit; it cannot be acquired by techniques or slick devices; 'faith' is a God-placed trust that needs not only the individual's response, but also the support of a life of fellowship and a sense of membership for its fuller display. These Christian words flourish in people's lives. They are not to be left imprisoned in the cold, black print of the dictionary. Nor are they for lip-service only. Literalism is not enough; when we mouth these words, we ask that God may be in our speaking.

Christ spoke more than he wrote. He had words for people, whether they were literate or illiterate. What he said came wonderfully alive among his hearers. We are right not to separate his sayings from the scenes of their utterance. The goodness of the sermon, or the counselling, or the argument, is found in the context of the event, at the particular moment of encounter. This is true also of the hard question and the good answer; it is true of the reason given for the faith of the believer.

The question 'Who is my neighbour?' produced an answer that is still remembered whenever the story of the good Samaritan is told. That parable with its good and powerful wording has changed much badness into goodness: words of this sort in action enrich and glorify much that is hopeful and promising in human life.

Simplicity of Speech

'What I have, that I give' (Acts 3:6). Peter's words to the lame beggar at the 'beautiful' gate of the temple in Jerusalem sounded simple enough.

Those words have been repeated through the centuries. They have echoed a deep truth about Christian communication in many an area of need. The simple words have a directness that might easily conceal the demand which they make upon the speaker. Many a missionary has translated those words into the language and dialect of those among whom the truths of Christianity have been shared. There is depth in the simplicity; those words of giving and healing were far from being simplistic. The effect has not been magical, although it may have been mysterious. Peter, with the words he uttered, gave himself, as he passed on generously to another what he had in turn received. The words were his in one sense for his faith in Jesus Christ was contained in them; in another way, they were words held in trust, not of his own invention, but communicated by him personally from one infinitely greater and more eloquent. This was an early example of the ministry of the word in the history of the young Christian Church.

In this conversation with the disabled man we hear only one half of the dialogue. Peter and John fasten their eyes on the anonymous beggar and selecting him for their attention and concern from among the crowd, they say to him, 'Look on us.' The beggar responds with an expectant look, and doubtless an accompanying gesture, prior to the receiving of the usual coin: then come the words 'Silver and gold have I none, but such as I have I give thee: in the name of Jesus Christ rise up and walk.' The currency of such speech had the value of a new authority, a power, if not to purchase, at any rate to comfort and restore. The psalm singer, long before, had expressed what he had learned through his spiritual studies: that the law of God's mouth is dearer to him than thousands of gold and silver pieces (Psalm 119:72).

If the gate of the temple was called Beautiful, certainly something beautiful for God shone through the squalor and poverty presented by this disfigured, degraded life, now healed. The business of apostles such as Peter and John was with the kind of words which were swiftly identified with deeds. The same Hebrew word is used for 'thing' and 'word'. The theorising and the opinions of the apostles were not to the fore in the early preaching and teaching. They dealt in the facts of faith. The record of their business was called 'The Acts of the Apostles', not their thoughts. If money could not buy the cure for the crippled patient, God's word certainly proved effective.

The apostles' work was factual. Words became events. Speaking as they were commissioned to speak resulted in happenings, not in endless talking. Those who heard them at their business of proclaiming the good news and speaking the language of the Spirit did not always perceive the source of their power. Simon the sorcerer who, in contrast to the apostles, had given out 'that himself was some great one' offered money in the hope of purchasing the power of the Apostles' words and deeds. 'Thy money perish with thee,' came the answer from Peter, 'because thou hast thought that the gift of God may be purchased with money: thou hast neither part nor lot in this matter; for thy heart is not right in the sight of God.'

Embarrassing in a different way was the reaction of the centurion Cornelius whose vision led him to fall down at Peter's feet and worship him (Acts 10). 'Stand up; I myself also am a man,' said Peter as he realised that this outsider was not to be excluded from the Christian community.

The boldness of speech of Peter and John impressed their hearers. These unlearned and ignorant apostles spoke the right words at the right time. The people 'took knowledge of them, that they had been with Jesus'.

Similar beautiful things for God are done in our day and spoken about in the simplest terms of God-talk. Mother Teresa of Calcutta is called upon to give an account of her work on public occasions, and to give reasons for attempting such a formidable task of loving care amid the ailing, ageing and poverty-stricken inhabitants of the large city. Her words are always simple, but strong. She tells us that God loves every one of the crowd, including the unloved and uncared-for. Those who, humanly speaking, are classed as incurable, are to be loved too. She helps the aged to die; she wants them to die well, not to die in loneliness and indignity. These lives are more precious than gold and silver in the eyes of the Almighty. The simple words of the early Church express the fundamentals of the faith.

A recent report by an African Christian leader, describing the life of his Church to an audience in London, contained repeated reminders of the acts of the first apostles. Simple words of faith had caused teachers and preachers to be imprisoned; out of scenes of conflict and tension, the straight speaking about love and justice and freedom which echoed the words of Jesus proved to be dangerous but victorious, at one and the same time.

'What I have, that I give' commits us all and, for all the simplicity of the words, the sentence makes far-reaching demands: service and fellowship, emerging from this attitude of generosity, and vitality and spiritual enrichment in ordinary lives.

The simple sentence 'What I have, that I give' turns the theory of loving and caring into compassionate action. There is no reserve attached to this offer; the price of love has no ceiling to set a limit to it. Peter, who spoke from the heart to the beggar, had himself been looked upon by his Master on a memorable occasion with a loving and longing gaze that produced in him a change of heart. It was a changed Peter that was now in a position 'to fasten his eyes' on a brother in need, and to ask for a returning look. He then saw the beauty, while others passed it by, unnoticing: he looked through the wounds to the healing. He gave, not what he had, but what he was. The simple words were living and active.

A Voice in the Wilderness

John the Baptist's voice gained a hearing. The cry from the wilderness, in his case, was not in vain. His role, as a forerunner of One who was to come, had a significance which marked him out from a babel of voices.

His voice sounded dramatically and memorably. Handel in his *Messiah* made the solo voice, singled out, all the more memorable, when he set to music of great beauty the trenchant message, ringing with authority.

The voice prepared the way. The preparation brought understanding and expectation. There were preliminary questions to be asked before Christ came. As the Baptist moved among the crowds, these questions were searching and pertinent: he observed the needs of the people. He had a word for each section of the community; he looked for a response from those who had special qualifications to offer through service, and personal contributions to make.

In our speaking, we utter sounds. The accent and the tone of speech reveal personality and betray feelings. 'A word fitly spoken' (Proverbs 25:11), 'is like apples of gold in pictures of silver.' Such words have power and influence as well as beauty and costliness.

Yet some words go unheeded. However earnestly we may pray that God should be in our speaking, we have no guarantee that we will be heard for our speaking, whether it be much or little. Sometimes we have to endure the loneliness and the pain of speaking words that go unheeded. Some truths, quaintly called home-truths, receive no listeners and earn no response, no applause. Home-truths should be communicated in love and affection; the words may cause the hearers to wince and smart; yet, subsequently, their meaning comes clear and their prophetic and remedial properties are seen to be productive.

Our voice may possibly be drowned by a chorus of opposing voices. One voice, still and small, has power to be heard above the din; after the thunder, lightning and fire the message gets through. Not loudness, nor vociferousness will gain the hearing, but prophecy, authority, sincerity, and authenticity will have the ring of truth.

A voice crying in the wilderness on certain historic occasions has won attention out of all proportion to its sound and its carrying power.

There was prophecy in this voice. John the Baptist was called the last of the prophets; he quoted the old traditional words of faith and interpreted them for the day in which he lived and made their meaning new. Everyone needed to hear the voice, for all had needs of some kind, whether they actually felt them or not. Penitence was necessary if the new life was to be received. It was difficult for some to appreciate that this was so. The voice, however, pierced the veils of complacency and self-sufficiency that covered up many countenances. The speech of the prophet challenged the listeners to be aware of other people's needs and to be sensitive to the conditions of life which those less fortunate had to endure, people to whom they had given little consideration.

A voice from outside, from a wilderness, distant and apart, is an independent voice, disinterested, freed from bias. Those who are caught up in life's ambiguities do well to listen to the critical, yet constructive, counselling given by one who was dedicated to the work of preparation for the future. The urgency of his cries of command may have suggested that he was the one for whom the world waited to rescue it from its confusion. The humility, however, of his open and candid speech enabled others to see themselves in their true colours and to look ahead for better news still. John said plainly and honestly that the time would come when he must decrease and another must increase. There was a vast difference between his message and the Man of whom he spoke. A single, minority voice can, in the context of a spiritual crisis or a great divine event, have an influence that defies calculation, if the sound is allowed to come out of the wilderness and to reverberate throughout the world.

John the Baptist came in the spirit and guise of an Elijah. When he spoke nought for his listeners' comfort, he found himself unpopular. Lashing with his tongue in the cause of righteousness, it seemed certain that an early martyrdom lay in wait for him. When death came and his head lay on a charger to satisfy a royal wish, his championing of the truth had already borne fruit.

Such martyrs do not die in vain, nor is their witness merely eccentric. Theirs is a vocation to unpopularity for the truth's sake. A popular prophet is a contradication in terms when a world is in need and its peoples are spiritually blind. Like Jonah, such a prophet is jettisoned from the ship; as with Cassandra from a different culture, the truth when spoken is mostly not believed.

Yet the right of the lone voice to be heard is one of the important liberties to be preserved in organised society. Athanasius was the only leader not in step during a long and controversial struggle for Christian truth and doctrinal orthodoxy. Spiritually in the wilderness, alone against his whole world, he exercised, from exile, an influence which ultimately prevailed. His minority view was credible and gained acceptance.

The pastor of Buchenwald, who gave his life in 1938 for an unpopular cause, appeared stubborn and unnecessarily obtuse, when he could have signed a paper to free himself from the confines of the concentration camp: yet in his person and through his faith he fought the issue of a world war before it was launched upon the nations. The spirit of the Baptist's cry on the banks of Jordan still encourages others 'constantly to speak the truth, boldly to rebuke vice, and patiently to suffer for the truth's sake'.

Living Speech

The 'word' of God is described in one of the psalms as a lantern. It gives light to the feet of the traveller as he moves along his pathway. It helps him to make progress in spite of the darkness and obstacles on the road. He who finds the word of God illuminating has his feet on the ground and is concerned with the present situation in which he is involved. The lantern is at his feet in the very spot where he is treading; it is true that the word of God is also a 'light' for the travellers' path and points a way ahead, looking to the immediate future.

We live in a world of words, written, spoken, recorded, relayed. We need to examine our vocabulary to see if the words are living and sparkling. Phrases easily become outworn, metaphors die, losing their life and colour. Statements about faith and morality need re-statement from time to time. In an age of slogans, myths, clichés, and tabloid answers to stock problems, pure speech is required to give life to our language.

A good word is a symbol of faith, honesty, and sincerity; again, bad language for the Christian is defeatist talk which drives out hope, and hypocritical utterances which build a barrage of words to cloud the real issues and to mask the speaker's inner thoughts and intended purpose.

In today's language of worship there is a welcoming renewal of phrase and a fresh vocabulary of faith and penitence. The world with its present-day needs is brought into the sanctuary, as it were; plain and unadorned is the place where God comes into the conversation of prayer. The straightforward talk of grateful sinners and willing servants adds intimacy to this kind of speaking with God. The naturalness and helpless ignorance of those who put into their own words their wishes and hopes give life to words of prayer. The 'you' of love and friendship replaces the more distant, more formal 'thou' in the current prayers of life offered to God.

Powerful Language

St Paul, in his letters, gained a reputation for candour. He meant what he wrote: his words of comfort and love emerged from his own inner conflict and the outer controversies which surrounded him in his work, wherever he went. He constantly turned for help to God whom he had come to trust through the vision of Jesus granted to him. He prayed that he might have on his lips the right words at the right moment, that he might open his mouth boldly, to speak as he ought to speak. His language was brave and strong, well-tested, and sincere. His sufferings and his personal spiritual experiences coloured his words.

Christian spirituality is often expressed in tough and sinewy words. Weapons from the armoury, famously described and listed by Saint Paul, have had a persisting influence upon the language of prayer. The panoply of sword and helmet, breastplate and greaves, is not as militaristic as it sounds. Nor is fighting the good fight crudely pugnacious. Nevertheless a spiritual combat continues realistically wherever there is human life, wherever the clash between persons, parties, and nations disturbs the peace and harmony 'which the world cannot give'.

Words are weapons. The sword of the spirit is a familiar term for the Word of God. So sharp and penetrating is this Word of God that the words that convey its power can bring order out of confusion and shed a bright light in a very dark corner of life.

Spirituality, therefore, has no flabbiness in its make-up. It is deeply concerned with the comforting of souls and the healing of sufferings, but its operation savours of struggle, not of softness or any soothing. Truth has to be upheld in the face of distortion of facts and the deceptions of the selfish. Champions of the truth are called upon to struggle to their feet and be counted. Their instruments of action include righteousness and faith; peace, also, is a weapon in the same struggle.

'They daily mistake my words,' wrote the psalmist in one of his spiritual songs written in loneliness, when he felt frustrated and misunderstood. At any period in history, such a sentiment is frequently expressed when there has been a breakdown in communication, and lines are crossed. This common experience of those whose business is with words serves as both a warning and a spur. We learn the hard way that good speech must be clear and strong, perhaps even rugged with an edge to it, before it can be flowing and effective. The poets who have emerged in the contemporary scene of struggle and conflict in Ireland express what few can state in words. Their choice of words declares the mystery of life. Their rhythm, also, conveys in phrases, often assonant and crystalline, experiences that defy precise expression. Artists in words reflect 'the tears of things' and remind us of the loneliness of spiritual endurance.

Spoken Words for Worship

Someone has counted up to thirty different phrases and expressions for 'worship' in the New Testament. Yet it is difficult to find among the languages of Europe an exact equivalent for the word 'worship'. 'Cult' will scarcely provide the answer. 'Worthiness' tells only part of the story. The word 'worship' in fact is an expression of love as well as of honour. Love produces life and action. If worship defies definition, it deserves analysis. The many words employed in the task of describing the single activity of worship illustrate the wide extent of the worshipper's response.

The Christians worshipped with their mind in the beginnings of the Church's life. They also listened to the word of God, read aloud in their company, when they met for prayer. This sitting and listening to the spoken word were characteristic of the worship of the Jewish synagogue. The Christians continued that method of meditation on passages of scripture; the listening to the sounds of the words, and the catching of the rhythms of poetry in psalm and prophecy became an important activity in their devotions. The quotations of Jesus from the Old Testament and the sayings of Jesus himself were passed on orally from mouth to mouth, and memorised. These became the subject of their thoughts and when received in this way through live speech they provided the content of their prayers of meditation. Doubtless, the fixed gaze and the tense hanging upon the words, when read aloud in their hearing, formed an important part of the communication by which their minds were fed. Worship, in a word, was described in that context as 'taking care' or 'giving heed'.

Poetry and Song

In the epistle to the Ephesians, we read of the Christians exhorted to address one another in psalms and hymns and spiritual songs. The psalms, used by Christ in his devotions, have become a staple diet in the life of prayer.

These psalms of Israel were for singing and worshipping. They supply words of praise, penitence, petition, and intercession for Christians at prayer, who find this popular expression of devotion fitting and lasting.

As songs of a people they have been closely associated with the musical instruments which provided accompaniments to the rhythms of the Psalter's language.

If the proverbs of the Bible, with their words of wisdom packed tightly into memorable phrases, are for reading and re-reading and meditation, then the psalms deserve repeated singing. They express themes of joy and thanksgiving; they are also psalms for all seasons and moods; the note of judgment and wrath sounds ominouly at intervals in the rich collection of devotion; penitence and anguish express the varying moods in human experience.

These songs have outlasted many of the passing favourites which have ascended, and then quickly descended, in popularity. Human needs and familiar tempers are to be found in this book of a people – a people who sensed that God was in their speaking; they had a sturdy faith and found much in their nation's history and their spiritual tradition for which to be thankful. They never seemed to tire of referring back repeatedly to great events which demonstrated God's care for them. His providence and guidance were constant themes.

From the earliest days of Christianity in Ireland, the psalms have been in circulation to aid the devotion and to mould the lives of those who learned them by heart and delighted in their sounds and themes. It is not surprising that a well-thumbed psalter survives from the days of St Columba, or Columb-kille. The so-called 'Battle Psalter', the *Cathach,* is a manuscript of fine writing, with capital letters of sensitive design, dating from the sixth century A.D., and now in the Library of the Royal Irish Academy in Dublin. Written with liturgical directions for use in the worship of the monastery, this psalter forms a link with the earliest traditions of Christian worship and the use of the psalms in the first days of the Church's life.

Jesus had used them from the days of his childhood, attending the synagogue, 'as his custom was', in his home town of Nazareth. Words from the psalms were in his mouth and in his speaking as he hung on the cross at Calvary. Words of agony and forsakenness came to his aid at an hour of near-despair; the psalms, too, provided words of trust and sure hope, when he commended his spirit into the hands of God at the last.

Psalms, also, had been sung by Jesus with his friends when after supper they went out to the mount of Olives. They recalled in the words of their song the overtones of the Passover's deliverance and the prophecies of Jesus' coming sacrifice.

The psalms do not rhyme in the manner of hymns and the stanzas of much poetry with which we are familiar. Their words, however, flow with a rhythm which creates fellowship and harmony. They were composed as songs; many of them had refrains with words which gathered mounting momentum. The enthusiasm of the repeated 'for his mercy endureth for ever' in psalm 136 is clearly cumulative; the crescendo is unmistakable. Such sound of music stirs life among the worshippers and wins from them a fervent response.

The theme of God speaking to his people runs through the Psalter continually. Even the difficult psalms which in fierce language and fiery tones express the stresses and anguish of those caught up in the conflict of their history, find a realistic place in these songs of trust. Admittedly, there are words and phrases hard to use in our own time.

Protest, as well as promise, is a feature of some psalms, as they sound their notes of sternness. The judgment of God, no less than his mercy, is reckoned with, and not weakly avoided. In sentences that are recited in parallel verses, the singer emphasises his convictions and then 'says it again' in different words, to underline his meaning, with contrasts and comparisons. 'The Lord knoweth the way of the righteous' asserts a firm belief that deserves emphasis with the power that a contrast is able to supply: 'but the way of ungodly shall perish.'

Here is dialogue. Here is food for argument and discussion. This vigorous communication expresses a well-tested spiritual experience. It was apparently not enough to make any mere casual reference to this matter of right and wrong. Let it be sung; let it be repeated in a memorable refrain and a pointed antithesis; let its significance be turned over and examined with all the thoroughness which this style of worship and speaking with God pungently provides.

There are also songs of deliverance in the Psalter; there are seasonal psalms, too, which help the harvest home. Such psalms sing of the glories and the hazards of nature. They relate all that we see and handle to the wisdom and ordering of God.

Those psalms that are personal give balance and proportion to the chorus of the songs designed for the crowded congregation. Sometimes a psalm is a lonely cry from the heart, in a low key, uttered 'out of the deep'. Even when eyes are lifted up to the hills, the spiritual and permanent help comes not from our surroundings, however beautiful the landscape, but from the Lord, who made heaven and earth.

The psalms were Jewish and remained part of the culture of the first Christians in Palestine; their words were woven into the early liturgies of the Church. Together with the psalms, Greek hymns enriched this worship, and the two cultures were blended. The imagery of light in such hymns as 'Hail, gladdening light' brought the victorious note of resurrection into the language of prayer and praise, supplementing gems of devotion from the prophecy of the psalms such as the rare versicle 'In thy light shall we see light' and the opening invocation 'O send out thy light and thy truth that they may lead me.'

The chorus-word 'Hallelujah,' which praised the Lord in the Psalter with acknowledgment of the many blessings granted through a nation's history, became the obvious word of praise, to be spoken or sung by those who declared that Christ was risen from the dead. Later, some famous music gave buoyancy to these praises. Handel and others perceived the immortality of these words from the mouths of believers in the resurrection. The endless Hallelujahs of the Church's song have fostered hope and sustained drooping spirits more effectively than many a sermon or credal statement.

Words without songs continue to express beliefs and prayers. Songs add wings to spoken words. They become moving vehicles of adoration and inspired praise. In the New Testament, we sense that the Christians were swift to respond to the invitation to sing with the spirit; and to sing with the understanding also.

Singing enriches speech and is seen to make more demands upon the whole person. Not only with their mouth and lips, but with full-throated voice and deeply drawn breath, the singers give joyfully and strenuously of themselves. Harmony and unison strengthen the fellowship and save it from dull monotony and a flat sameness.

Today many songs of faith are happily shared across the divisions of Christendom. In the week of prayer for Christian unity, now established as a regular event in the life of the Churches each January, music and singing have played a significant part when words of hymns and pslams and spiritual songs were shared.

This sharing of words in prayer and song has been a welcome feature on special days of intercession for peace in times of violence and conflict. Worship, organised in the market place and similar open spaces, has created a new kind of fellowship among those unaccustomed to joining in prayer with the representatives of such a diversity of traditions. 'The Lord is my shepherd', the twenty-third psalm, in poetry or prose, provides on such occasions much welcome common ground; there is relaxation, free from self-consciousness, and the tune Crimond binds the worshippers together.

In this way, all Christians, in spite of their differences, discover their common heritage.

Words of Controversy

Words, of course, often bring division. This has to be recognised by those who endeavour to act together where possible, without hurt to their consciences. So far from communicating thoughts and intentions, some words which smack of ancient controversy are so contentious that they foster violent moods and rash intolerance. Added to this, the manner of the speaking and uttering of words of faith turns them at times into slogans and catch-cries too contentious to be charitable. The prayer 'God be in my mouth' becomes urgent for us in our speaking if eagerness for the opportunity to express our own dearly held conviction drives from our words and the tone of them the spirit of charity without which we are nothing. We think of the famous words written in a very different age, but pointed and powerful for Christians today when they speak to each other: 'I may be able to speak the languages of men and even of angels, but if I have no love, my speech is no more than a noisy gong or a clanging bell. I may have the gift of inspired preaching; I may have all knowledge and understand all secrets; I may have all the faith needed to move mountains – but if I have no love, I am nothing.'

Words of controversy are receiving deeper consideration in

the current dialogue among the separated Churches. A re-statement of belief is not to be equated with a lessening of conviction or an abandoning of principle. Words such as 'saved' and 'lost', 'heresy' and 'schism', at certain periods in Christian history guarded precious truths of the faith. Today they merit re-examination and fresh expounding among the Churches who have discovered in their speaking together many words about God's love and justice which they can happily share.

Words from the Scriptures, shared after study and frank discussion, have a significant part in healing the sores of controversy. Phrases from the New Testament concerning 'authority', 'the spirit', 'communion', and 'unity', to mention but a few, become subjects about which the truth must be spoken in love. Such speaking, relying on the grace and guidance of the three-personed God, reveals areas of both agreement and disagreement, and yet it has been found that, in the differences, understanding is created and love is not damaged by hostile pride or jealousy. Such are the standards and aims of ecumenical speaking. The keen champions of the faith and the honest searchers after truth are not lulled into the sleep of indifference in such an atmosphere of good-will. The candour and clarity of divided Christians speaking together with charity serve to create both a mood of repentance and a spirit of renewal at one and the same time. With these necessary preliminaries, the accredited representatives of the several Churches listen to the God who speaks.

It is heartening to find the Churches speaking to one another. There are many divisions among Christians, but their mutual contacts are steadily increasing. Not long ago, the spire and the tower in the towns and villages of Ireland seemed to express in permanent stone a tension and a great divide in the community. They still indicate a separateness, a distinction in ways of life. Yet a newly discovered relationship has brought a fresh vision to many who sense that they are not only citizens together, but also fellow-Christians.

For longer than anyone living can remember there have been friendships and courtesies. Good neighbours have not allowed the religious divide to spoil ordinary human exercises in cooperation. More recently a common ground of faith has been recognised and openly spoken about. Common standards of outlook and behaviour have drawn whole congregations, and not merely individuals, into a new kind of relationship.

Prayer together seemed unthinkable a few years ago. Times of suffering and distress have undoubtedly played an important part in this new urge to share in the things of the spirit. A spontaneity in these combined efforts for closer fellowship seemed to indicate that Christ himself triumphs over all our divisions and through him an essential unity shines through the obvious, but sincerely held, differences. There is less inclination to look back or to live in the past. The times in which we find ourselves stimulate the search for life's meaning and purpose as we move forward together and sense that we are dependent upon one another.

Differences appear even in our speaking with God in prayer. It is a cause of gratitude that the family prayer with its intimate address, 'Our Father', is a treasure widely shared, even if the family is evidently not unanimous. In earlier days, the similarity of the prayer used by all sorts of Christians was often only grudgingly recognised. In the English versions a fuss was made over the 'who' or the 'which' in the clause that followed the opening 'our Father', and the various traditions were jealously guarded with a literalness that sometimes expressed a distinction without a difference. No longer is it the general view that a common text spells treachery; there is the more generous thought that divided Christians on certain occasions can share a single Christ in their speaking and praying.

An ancient prayer, used in the season of Easter, puts the point when it asks that all those 'who are admitted into the fellowship of Christ's religion may eschew those things that are contrary to their profession and follow all such things as are agreeable to the same'. This fellowship of Christ's religion gains in credibility when Christians are honest with one another, not shirking the difficulties, nor yet shrinking from treading on common ground.

Translating Words and Meanings

Those devoted linguists who in many periods of Christian history have set their hand to translate the Bible, deserve the gratitude of the present-day followers of Jesus Christ in all the Churches and throughout the world. The earliest translation work was carried out by Greek-speaking Jews in Egypt. They began translating the Old Testament into Greek in Alexandria in the middle of the third century B.C. Called after the seventy, or more accurately the seventy-two, who worked separately for seventy-two days and (so the story runs!) produced identical translations at the end, this Greek version is known as the Septuagint, the Seventy. The fantastic account of their achievement illustrates the human reluctance to accept a translation which might appear to break with tradition or to process too individualistic a style.

This reluctance is still evident today, even if the business of translation is less picturesque. On balance, however, the versions of recent decades have been welcomed for the vividness of their language and the freshness given to the old truths. Words of ordinary, current speech have presented the message of the Scriptures with clear-cut expressions and crisp phrasing, free of archaisms.

It is regrettable that quoting from the Bible has been made more difficult and is more confusing. Understandably the words of the 'Authorised' Version of King James have still a respected and treasured place in English literature; its words have a particular dignity and beauty; they wear well and merit frequent quotation, for they add a richness to everyday speech which we can ill afford to lose.

A compromise is often observed, and there are many readers who use both the older and the more recent versions together, making comparisons and cross-references to add to their appreciation and enjoyment of the spirit of the writings. They recall that much of the Scriptures stemmed from oral traditions, passed from mouth to mouth, before being recorded in writing.

Translators, so far from being traitors, have a place with teachers in communicating the living word. Preachers and missionaries also find themselves in partnership with them when faced with the increasing demands made by educated and discerning readers for an accurate and authentic interpretation of what was seen and heard concerning Jesus Christ.

It is quite apparent that of the making of many biblical translations 'there is no end'. Since the Scriptures contain living words it is not surprising that the language in which they are understood is expected to be lively and contemporary.

The record of Jesus Christ's life and work was set down in the Greek of the New Testament. The Greek of the period was in common use and many meanings in the gospel narrative have been made clear by reference to correspondence on business and family matters surviving from papyri, preserved in the sands of Egypt. The word for 'daily' bread in the Lord's Prayer appears to have been used for a recognised 'ration' of food in the jargon of these times.

Again, the style of the Greek in the New Testament is sometimes literary, lucid, beautifully expressed, but not now spoken. St Luke provides us with examples of artistry in words, not only in the introductory words of his gospel, but also in the fine descriptive powers he displays as he records the parables and speeches of Jesus. There is evidence, also, in the gospel according to St John that the limitations of language and of the written word in conveying the atmosphere and spirituality of the good news of the kingdom of God are frankly admitted. At the end of this fourth gospel the author explains the problem: 'There are also many other things which Jesus did: were everyone of them to be written, I suppose that the world itself could not contain the books that would be written.'

The beautiful cadences of the 'Elizabethan' English of some translations of the Scriptures, including the Authorised Version of King James, live for us not through the printed word alone, but also in the voice of the reader and the interpretation of the musical composer. The words woven into liturgy or matched with the music of the oratorios sustain their inspiration over centuries with a kind of timelessness.

Side by side with these cultured and artistic expressions of the words of faith, it is well to remember the down-to-earth principles adopted by Martin Luther when he faced the task of translating the Scriptures into the vernacular, into speech which ordinary, unsophisticated people could understand. Luther was not content with a single and final version of the Bible, but saw the need for continuing revision. The living word demanded such currency.

In his day Luther revealed that he did not consult the academics, whose speech was Latin, in order to seek advice about the words and style which he should adopt for his translation: 'We must ask', he wrote, 'the mother in the home, the children on the street, the common man in the market-place about this, and look them in the mouth to see how they speak and, afterwards, do our translating.'

Today, with the battle for literacy, translation carries the faith into life with increasing energy and urgency. Rapid communication and ever more frequent interchange of news and views have introduced into our speech short-hand expressions, and crisply, freshly-minted words and phrases. ·

The Revised Standard Version's translating committee has adopted Luther's approach and still remains in session for its continuing work. The Revised Standard Version was published some forty years ago; its team of scholars is drawn from varied Christian traditions; its ecumenical character has given this version a notable status and has won wide acceptance. To quote Bruce Metzger, the committee's chairman, 'For the first time since the Reformation, one edition of the Bible has the blessing of the Protestant, Roman Catholic and Eastern Orthodox Churches alike.' The volume is entitled 'The Revised Standard Version of the Bible with the Apocrypha'.

For discussion, meditation, and daily inspiration, a modern version such as The Good News Bible, in a language disturbingly pointed and sometimes alarmingly unambiguous, involves more and more readers and moves them to Christian action and a new commitment to their message. Not only the words, but the presentation of them in readable form with clear head-lines to mark the paragraphs, encourages the reading and hearing public to find here the good news of God.

Chapter IV

'God be in my heart and in my thinking'

Jesus taught in parables. He made his listeners think. Sometimes those who heard him were baffled, and expressed the wish that he might talk plainly, and not in parables. Yet the parables carried the message in terms which have lasted through centuries. They made their point, and not just for the moment, at a particular place, for those hearers who had gathered to listen. There was spiritual food here for many generations.

Truth Embodied in a Story from Life

'A certain man made a great supper.' This dramatic opening sentence introduces a parable that is neither a sermon nor an exhortation urging the people who were listening to be good. Nor yet is it a piece of reasoned argument about a spiritual truth. There is no doubt, however, that the story of the great supper fascinated the audience and made them all think.

Christ's parables as often as not administered a shock. Obscure in meaning, and mysterious in idiom, these illustrations from human life and nature provided inexhaustible material for deep thinking.

When Jesus spoke plainly, his disciples noticed at once the change in his teaching method and said, 'Now you speak plainly and speak no parable.' Yet the parable or proverb or word-picture riveted his hearers' attention upon him, as he told the story, and upon the details that made the plot vivid and memorable.

When Jesus spoke plainly, he was often met with a barrage

of interruptions, words of abuse, and even showers of stones. Parables, however, were heard to the end, while the listeners hung on his words. He carried them with him; he captured their attention and gave them food for thought. Certainly parables about the Kingdom and the suffering which his passion would involve were received in the silence of reflection and deep emotion. These parables opened up a vision of life. The word-pictures which presented scenes from everyday living disclosed the deeper meaning of life. Parables also stirred thoughts and prompted questions.

There had been a hint given about the purpose of the parable as a teaching form or a means of communication, 500 years before Christ, when God's people were destined to have a strange mission and an unusually eccentric calling. They were told, 'thou shalt become an astonishment, a proverb or a parable, and a by-word among all nations whither the Lord shall lead thee.' (Deuteronomy 28:37).

It is notoriously difficult to help home a spiritual or moral truth. Acceptance for a right judgment is not always most successfully won by straightforward exhortation. Accurate statements about abstract principles of right and wrong often fail to win agreement. Platitudes or glimpses of the obvious have not the power to move the mind and will. Yet truth is often illuminated when hidden in a paradox or embodied in the tale of a human conflict. Our Lord spoke in parables, not for the sake of obscurity, although it was evident that some of his hearers found him obscure. They listened, but failed to grasp the point. What he presented in this form proved far more penetrating and profound than the precepts and statutes of the moral teaching of his day. He addressed in parables those who were steeped in the conventional language of religion and morality. They knew their duties, line upon line. They could recite their ordinances. The parables, however, shook them from their complacency and stirred them from fixed and rigid positions. The story of the great supper, for example, caught their imagination and gave them something to worry about, as they examined themselves and made fresh judgments in the light of the points it made.

A parable is more than an illustration or a simile. In a few sentences it can give a vivid picture of one range of life in order to throw light upon a different range. The speaker in parables is a creative artist; Jesus also had a prophetic authority as he spoke of a future which he saw clearly. His parables both persuade the listeners and also divide them. They pronounce judgments upon behaviour. They catch the conscience of an audience. They illustrate with an ingenious penetration the qualities of the new life in the kingdom of God. 'The great supper' teaches in arresting terms a lesson about the loyalty required of all those who belong to the kingdom. The parable causes us furiously to think about the generous and, at first sight, undeserved, welcome extended to all who will join the fellowship of reconciliation and love, without the usual tests and qualifications.

From the Heart

It is quite possible to talk about religion without being particularly religious. There is a jargon, a current vocabulary, which expresses the accepted beliefs; but the words spoken may be mere linguistics. It is equally possible to be deeply religious without uttering a syllable from the literature of devotion and piety. In spite of the risk, however, of being known either as a hypocritical babbler, or even as too religious for words, the Christian with an honest and good heart sees how increasingly important it is for him today to speak articulately 'out of the abundance of his heart'.

There is no lack of theorising and speculation about religious matters. Apocalyptic and prophetic writings abound in these uncertain and perilous days. Wrong beliefs appear tantalisingly attired in almost the same dress as right beliefs, to the dismay of the orthodox Christian. Words about the end of the world, the next crisis, the truth of biblical prophecy, can easily sound plausible, even if they are actually fantastic. The words of Christian vocabulary, if not used with care, become rapidly frozen, isolated from contemporary thinking, and obsolete. Our minds need to be stocked with words which not only sound right but possess meaning that find expression in a living and changing style and idiom.

The Word in the biblical sense is a creative, powerful thing. Those who have rediscovered this call the Word dynamic. Word and Action in the setting of faith go together. 'God spake the Word, and they were made': 'he commanded and they were created.' Christ's word worked results. 'Say but a word and my servant shall be healed' was the remark of one who trusted the speaker as well as the speaker's words. Christ, in fact, was the Word, the meaning of everything in heaven above and in earth beneath. 'Such knowledge is too wonderful and excellent for me; I cannot attain unto it,' sang the psalmist with prophetic anticipation.

Ever since Christ ascended, and Christian theology began to be expressed in technical terms, there has been a difficulty about stating in words all that we know and believe about the Word. It is not hard to understand why. The point about Christianity is that Christ was once for all proclaimed at a certain period in history, but he must be preached in every land and in every age in terms that are living and developing. New thinking on unchanging truth claims our hearts and minds.

The poetry which conveys biblical truths about God and the world is a more lasting vehicle of meaning than many passing sermons which have attempted in their day to define with accuracy and precision something that cannot adequately fit a formula or be set down in writing. So we rejoice to have the parable and the proverb to stock our minds and guide our thinking as we express our own thoughts in terms that we admit are temporary, inadequate, and fumbling, yet have become part of ourselves and our believing.

Peace of Mind

When God is in our thinking, he gives peace and wholeness to the random thoughts of our minds and the turbulent emotions of our hearts.

This peace of mind is peace with a difference. Peace of mind spells inward integration; distinct from pieces of mind, with accompanying distractions, restlessness, and gnawing discontent. Peace of mind is found by those whose minds are

stayed 'on God'. Peaceful minds are r
dumbfounded minds, divided this wa
temptations, doubts, and worries. The tru
won when the race is run and the prize forgo
is lost in the service of him who has the mast

All through his life Jesus was a peacem
appeared to stir up strife and murmurings, although
paradoxically he maintained that he came not to bring peace
but the cutting edge of division. In his work of healing, by his
words of forgiveness, through the strong calm of his patience
and humility, he earned the title 'Prince of Peace'. At his
command, the wind and waves were still; at his word the
struggling, writhing demon was expelled; by his silences in the
dock before his accusers and in his courageous, trustful death,
he revealed the power of peace.

The peace which passes understanding comes from God. It
is found, not without a struggle, by those who venture forth on
a long voyage of trusting, searching, and loving. Everyone who
would be guided into the way of peace must wrestle with self-
will and find through prayer and thought the truth of the poet
Dante's perfect summary of our relationship with God, 'In his
will is our peace.'

A Questioning Generation

Wrestling with problems and searching for truth raise
questions for the heart and mind. The leader of a boys' club in
Edinburgh had a brilliant way of dealing with the incessant
questions of the eager and often turbulent members. He
invited the most highly qualified team of experts that he could
find to write considered and satisfying answers to the
adolescent queries. The results were published in a series of
volumes and *Asking them Questions* makes stimulating
reading for all who have felt disturbed by the simple, oft-
recurring and yet penetrating questions posed by those who
are growing in wisdom and stature. The answers doubtless
helped the questioners; they also enabled us to observe the
train of thought pursued by the specialists, who nobly
expressed the fruits of their scholarship in non-academic

s, in popular language, freshly expressed for the needs of
boys' club.

Questions loomed large in the ministry of Christ. He wrote
no book that can be referred to. He framed no written laws.
Through questions which challenged and stirred, he imparted
much of his teaching with a lively freshness. In this way, he
encouraged not only deeper thinking but commitment to a
new outlook and a changed way of life.

Some of his questions were of the most practical and
detailed kind. 'How many loaves have you?' he asked on a
memorable occasion. Other questions would surprise and
challenge his hearers who had engaged him in conversation or
dispute; Christ would take the argument into deeper waters
than they had bargained for: 'Whose is this image and
superscription?', 'What think ye of Christ?' are among the
questions which looked for decisions. Sometimes the inquirers
were put off asking any more questions. The question once
asked, 'Will you also go away?' contained a judgment within
itself. There was also an uncomfortable question that surely
lingered in the minds of those that heard it: 'When the Son of
Man comes', Christ had asked, 'shall he find faith upon the
earth?' There was something searching, shaming, and sad in
the prophetic tone of such a challenge.

The Christian is called upon to think. He will expect to have
questions put to him by God and man. He must think things
out for himself. He cannot always provide a slick, neat answer,
as though word for word from a text-book. A Chestertonian
positiveness is, of course, wonderfully refreshing with its
incisive clarity amid the whirl of woolly wordiness that is all
too prevalent. The best answers are of the kind which involve
the one who replies with a new responsibility; such answers
are given not only with the lips but with the whole life.

We might be excused for thinking that today there are too
many questions in the air. The craze for much curious,
sometimes useless, information rages on. Some are the idle,
even irrelevant, questions of the busybody, others are genuine
queries from people puzzled and perplexed. Perhaps the
deepest questions concerning suffering, death, and the
hereafter will continue to be asked, always, and never be fully

answered. The posers from the boys' club demanded not only the expert accuracy of the specialist, but also the sympathy of the fellow-questioners, combined with the clarity and certainty of faith.

Battle for the Mind

'God be in my thinking' is a prayer for right conduct as well as for sound reasoning. The Spirit filled the heart and mind of Jesus when, in his temptations, he was given grace and light to proclaim his convictions with power and commitment.

The people of ancient Corinth, that city of allurements, were assured by St Paul that God would not allow them to be tempted beyond their ability to resist. He would make with the temptation a way of escape.

A way of escape, provided by the Almighty, sounds somewhat startling and quite out of character. We soon see, however, that the phrase about escaping does not suggest a kind of funkhole. Nor does it encourage that well-known disease of escapism, the shirking of an issue. The escape pointed to a solution, and a way through. No moral lapse need be regarded as incurable; there is a remedy for spiritual failure. No personal entanglement need be regarded as a trap from which there is no release. No path we tread, however crooked, is a cul-de-sac, too narrow to allow room for turning. On the contrary, courses adopted in life often help personal gifts to develop. Thus the soul progresses not in spite of difficulties and temptations, but because of them.

If we wish to find this way out and on, when in a moral quandary, we need to foster within our hearts 'the spirit to think and do always such things as be rightful'. The way out of temptation is best found positively. We move on to new ground; we make definite counter-decisions in the face of what so easily besets us. There is no apparent way out for those who believe that temptation does not exist, those who, head in sand, do not heed the warning signals and the reflexes which, when heeded, fore-arm both flesh and spirit. We need to have our head 'in our heart'.

Temptation demands analysis. Its sources vary, if we think

about it. Its modes of operation are deceptive. Sometimes its causes are entirely imaginary.

Starting in the mind, the temptation to worry about what might be rather than about what is can lead to moral confusion and even mental breakdown.

Doubts which have no foundation are too often treated with the respect due to long-established beliefs; they can introduce a loss of nerve and cause a person to hate his work and abandon his friends.

There is a temptation also which produces pride and blinds the heart; such is the temptation, not of the Pharisee, but of the publican who might have cared to be known as an interesting sinner, if he had not been patently and miserably penitent in the parable: 'I can resist everything except temptation,' said the character in *Lady Windermere's Fan*. The temptations of the mature include cynicism and complacency; they are just as menacing as the adolescent's temptations, and often far more difficult to combat. Deep-rooted becomes the constant inclination to appear independent of the world and its opinion, to live on a past reputation. The laurels of earlier achievements fade and grow limp when their winner has rested on them too long. The youthful temptations, which throw a personality off-balance for a period when passions are stormy and blood is hot, are easier to remedy by counselling and reasoning together than are the nagging, besetting disturbances of mind and spirit that linger and resist diagnosis.

The Christian life may be viewed in terms of repeated conflict with such trials of personality and character. Our Lord faced his tempter: each suggestion made to him was positively and decisively dealt with. His clear mind discerned the exact point at which the apparently right, and certainly most plausible, course was recommended – for the wrong reason. Jesus made his decisions without any compromise, without casting an eye upon quick results. He was dedicated to the task of interpreting the rightness of an action. Its rightness in the beginning, in the middle, and at the end, was his concern. Such action must also have pure motive and true purpose. The Christian, including the most disciplined ascetic, cannot expect to escape temptation. The battle for the mind and soul is on all the time. He can never avoid the issue but he can find a way through it. To meet every sin an opposite and overwhelming virtue must be advanced, if spiritual progress is to be made.

The obvious temptations may not be at the root of many spiritual disorders. Thus the recognition of a temptation is part of the heart-searching we need. Just as one man's meat can be another's poison, so one person's temptation is often subtly and sharply different from the next person's.

Our Lord's temptations were clearly not the obvious ones which beset the ordinary citizen. Yet we would be foolish to dismiss them on the grounds that they were not important for us to think about. His perfect life convinces us of his special temptations, as soon as we become accustomed to the thought that he was tempted at all in the same manner as we are. We are reminded that temptation is very different from sin. We are aware that the facing of danger and the running of risks expose us to the faults of cowardice and rashness; we take heart also, from the knowledge that the good and the upright among our acquaintances are exposed to temptations of no mean order, in their efforts to maintain the highest standards in their work and life. Much more inspiration still we find, therefore, in the spiritual history of the sinless Christ; his temptations did not appeal to any self-interest or personal satisfaction, but to his sense of service, his altruism, and his love for a world he had been called to rescue and redeem.

It used to be said in the life of the Church that clever people with sharp intellects were tempted to express heretical, and highly individual, opinions, because of their mental gifts. Such leaders of thought saw several steps ahead of the rest, and yet were often drawn into the exaggerations and eccentricities of half-truths. Their zeal misled them at times into fanaticism.

The good, as well as the clever, have also been tempted in the course of history to work alone, separating themselves from those who do not share their standards and ideals. They aim in this exclusive way to achieve their results more quickly. Impatient for ready answers, they have at times been led into excessively narrow fields of action. The abruptness of their good intentions has caused failures; the major problems in human life are generally solved in the long term, with patience and affliction playing their agonising part in the process.

The Heart's Core

'God be in my heart,' we pray. The words express the desire that God should be central in our life, our thinking, and our motives. Just as from the heart evil ideas come (Matthew 15:19) so it is important that the things of God and his righteousness should replace the ill-will and the apathy in the centre of our being and longings.

The collect of purity in the communion service, addressed to 'Almighty God to whom all hearts are open, all desires known, and from whom no secrets are hidden', sets the worshipper in the frame of mind which invites God in.

'May the words of my mouth and the thoughts of my heart be always acceptable in thy sight, O Lord my strength and my redeemer,' so runs a familiar invitation to start us thinking.

We think on the things which are God's – whatsoever is true, noble, right, pure, lovely and honourable. To have the mind of Christ is the aim of our meditation. Dwelling on these things transforms us. 'Do not conform yourselves to the standards of this world,' wrote St Paul, 'but let God transform you inwardly by a renewing of your mind, then you will be able to know the will of God – what is good and is pleasing to him and is perfect' (Romans 12:2).

The Eastern Orthodox tradition has much to teach us about the prayer of the heart. The publican in the parable pours out his heart, 'God, be merciful unto me a sinner,' penitence, shame, courage, humiliation pour from him. With that prayer, like the 'Jesus' prayer of the easterns, there is poured into the heart instead such love towards God that the worshipper, 'loving him above all things', may obtain the gracious promises which exceed all that we can desire.*

In his *Art of Prayer*, Theophan the Recluse advises, 'You

---

* 'The Jesus Prayer' is a short prayer which can be used at any time or in any place. Its words 'Lord Jesus Christ, Son of God, have mercy on me, a sinner,' often repeated, take all who use it to the heart of the gospel. It serves both as an act of worship and also as a means of holding our attention in the presence of God.

must not pray only with words, but with the mind, and not only with the mind, but with the heart, so that the mind understands clearly what is said in words, and the heart feels what the mind is thinking.'

Praying is Thinking

Prayer is a kind of thinking. Thoughts pass into prayer when we meditate and through our faith unite our desires and our hopes with God's will. 'I sometimes think about the Cross' and that thought becomes a contemplation.

We do not cease to think when we pray. We ask that our thinking may be disciplined and shared by God. We bring every thought into captivity to the obedience of God.

Prayer activates the mind. We recall a thought of Pascal's that we could not seek God unless he had already found us. For God to be in our thinking is essential, if a prayer is to be genuine and authentic.

Thinking engenders loving, willing, thanking, worshipping. We think of God not with detachment when we pray but with affection, finding ourselves personally committed to his way and his will.

We think of God in personal terms. Thinking is being in tune with his attributes. We say 'thou' to God. His is a living presence. Out of the abundance of the heart, the mouth addresses him. We do not refer to God in abstract, neutral, terms – our prayer is through Jesus Christ our Lord. Without the mediation of Christ, our thoughts would flounder.

To think of God is to remember his marvellous acts. These saving acts through history reveal God's nature and person.

Reflecting on his mercy and loving-kindness is also a way of thanking him and praising him. We think of our creation, preservation, and all the blessings of this life – just as Edward Reynolds felt, when he composed his prayer of General Thanksgiving under physical stress.

Prayer is a priority before decisions are faced and the smallest Christian action undertaken.

When saying Grace before meals, we think of the needs of others, the hungry and the homeless. As we think, we thank.

We think from the heart with feeling and compassion. It requires imagination to envisage other people's needs and what they are called upon to endure. We learn something of this from the beginnings of the Leprosy Mission which were small and humble. The thought that stirred the founder was 'cradled in prayer'; it sprang from the heart and was developed while compassion for neglected, unwanted, unhealthy sufferers persisted. Leprosy was a disease, but it was in fact people suffering from the disease who drew the sympathy of our Lord. All such, who have dropped out of society and are despised and rejected, are people for whom Christ died.

Similarly the Samaritan touch, which has brought personal caring in a practical way into the lives of the lonely and troubled, has revealed the power of the Christian ministry 'of the heart'. The watchers by the telephone in their round-the-clock vigil have rescued many from suicide and break-down since this imaginative Samaritan ministry began. Now, through a listening service in many countries, the spiritual guidance received by the bewildered and desperate callers has changed their thinking and, in many cases, restored or kindled a faith by which they are able to face life.

This 'heart to heart' talking, which the founder, Chad Varah, initiated, has been seen to have special importance among those who can no longer bring themselves to communicate with friends and counsellors 'face to face'. Their loneliness and suffering have been creative only after the agony of feeling abandoned and reaching the end of the resources of will and thought. 'God comes into their thinking' with the help of unknown, unnamed, invisible counsellors who bring relief and compassion to the sores which have brought thinking and hoping to a standstill. The need for this kind of counselling arises from the swiftly changing social conditions where cities are crowded and neighbourhoods have become strangely impersonal. Those who live near to one another are often unseen and unknown. The 'Samaritans' in their selfless service fill the many gaps that have been found in uncommunicative surroundings. They have been good listeners. They have heard many cries of despair. When they have lifted the receiver, they have found themselves entering a world of crisis and confusion, at the centre of which the anonymous caller is trapped.

These listeners have found, as they listened and began to understand the background of such personal suffering, that a spirit of patience and compassion can be transmitted to a caller in countless different ways. Thus confidence can be restored, and new lines of thought initiated, not with advice expressed in words, and certainly not with admonitions, but with the sympathy and rapport which the experienced and dedicated listener offers. The tone of voice, the warmth of welcome, the strength of faith contribute to this reverence for a life in distress.

The manner rather than the matter of the telephonic replies gives courage to those who were diffident, mistrusting others as well as themselves. A friendly murmur can be sufficient to give new assurance to the would-be speaker. For the despairing and the confused, any words to reflect their mood or express their innermost throughts have too often been hard to find.

The despairing have at last found an ear that will hear them. No one before this seemed to have had time to listen. Those who had heard the story with all its complexities, its misfortunes mingled with mistakes, had always failed to understand.

The signals of distress had not been seen in time. Their nearest and dearest had been too closely entangled, emotionally and personally, to be able to think clearly about the causes and the consequences of the problem.

This voluntary service, prompted by a love for people and a desire to help, is seen as prayer-in-action. Those who are Christian and have thought out their part in this healing of the mind and all that is meant by rehabilitation, find that their role of go-between is doomed to superficiality and merely temporary ambulance service, unless God is in the treatment and his love is seen as the power behind the service.

This most individual prayer 'God be in my thinking' reminds us that individuals are persons. Anonymous callers are people. Often unloved people, with resentment in their hearts against themselves and society, they need nothing more at times than some sign that another cares about them. They want to be treated as real persons. In some way, they want to be loved. This human service has stirred Christians to perceive more generously the needs that exist in their own vicinity. They can then bring into more active circulation the compassion they share with Jesus for the crowd, which he looked upon as a flock of sheep without a shepherd.

The listeners learned to think again as they heard the stories of agony, tragedy, and plain hard luck. Those in trouble never discover how much they help the helpers. Sometimes the callers found that, with a sympathetic listener who spoke little, they were answering their own questions before the receiver was finally replaced at the end of the story. The counsellors with their ears to the receivers often drew inspiration from their own thinking, their background of experience, their spiritual insights, and their own humility. At both ends of the conversation, caller and receiver listened and learnt; it is not hard to believe that their faithful creator was present at many such meeting-points of mind.

Such a listening ministry can be exercised at many levels. The light thrown upon the passion of Christ by the listeners who volunteer as committed Christians, aids our thinking about the mystery of suffering.

In Christian devotion, Cross and Passion are linked together. Likewise, Agony and Bloody Sweat add realism as well as ruggedness to much soul-searching which ought not to be ignored or toned down with any misplaced regard for delicacy.

Crucifixion may well have been a common occurence in the time of Jesus. In those turbulent days, we discern through the passion narrative that the cry 'Crucify him' was a popular outburst against many a criminal. Yet the special case of Jesus, condemned to this particular fate, gave prominence to the causes of the death and the claims of the victim. The Passion for Christians provides the key to the death. The death of Jesus is believed to have altered the character of death itself. Death for the Christian now means 'going where the Son of God has gone'.

So we think about the uniqueness of the event, as we ponder on its purpose and give thanks for its effect. The sin surrounding all that happened even appeared to be fortunate on account of 'the happy issue' out of all the affliction endured. Human suffering was to be viewed in a new light; yet suffering unfortunately and miserably continues amongst us.

What has been called 'the divine depth of suffering' deserves our examination. 'The double palm of humility and power' joined in one wreath by the crucified Christ claims our thoughts as we contemplate the bitterness of the Passion when, in a famous phrase by one whose thoughts on pain have helped many a sufferer, 'Jesus took the thorns and twisted them into a crown of glory'.

Strangely enough, fellowships of suffering have been repeatedly created among those who in heart and mind have found strength to follow the way of the Cross. This has been the consistent experience of those called upon to suffer in the past decade in our own island. Families which shared bereavement have been drawn close to one another; introduced to each other for the first time, when similar tragedies struck the several members, love and respect grew from the shattering and the shock. Those who were bereaved and seemed to have been most worthy of pity and sympathy, took the initiative in helping others with similar stories to tell of their suffering, so that the suffering together, which is at the heart of compassion's true meaning, might become productive of new life and strong hopes for facing the future. The sufferers were the first to bear one another's burdens and so to fulfil the law of Christ, who died that we might live. His sacrifice was not loss, but gain, not waste of life, but an offering of a total, perfect love.

It is reported from scenes of affliction and continuing poverty and distress in many of the developing countries that Christians find inspiration in a special way from the Passion of Christ and the celebration of the events of Holy Week, with the sort of emphasis that we give to Christmas and its accompanying atmosphere of good-will and happiness. Out of the crucible of all the pain, poverty, suffering, and personal degradation, a sense of solidarity is found. The old prayer 'passion of Christ, strengthen us' is more in tune with their longings and heart-searchings than can be found in the words of many a popular, Christmas carol.

Christ's sufferings are, of course, seen as different from much human suffering, yet he is recognised as one who is with the poor and the rejected, to love them and to care for them. He who suffered and yet retained his dignity, his integrity and his love unsullied, refusing to become bitter or disillusioned, has been in a remarkable way able to bring comfort and the kind of sympathy that shares the path of others and brings them the hope of rescue and healing.

There was no self-pity in the kind of suffering that Jesus endured. He did not complain of what fate or nature or fellow human beings brought upon him. Nor did he count among his disadvantages and hardships any economic problems from the days in the carpenter's shop.

His awareness of injustice, his concern for the unloved, his longing for many more to understand the truth and goodness of God were the sources of his pain and suffering. These things caused him to feel the passion of righteous indignation as well as sorrow of heart.

Christ's miseries were different from those experienced by 'the publicans and sinners' with whom he consorted. They found consolation in knowing that he was at their side and supportive when they repented. They perceived that he had no favourites.

For their sakes, as well as for all the rest, he became poor that they, through his poverty, might become rich. The riches included the expenditure of loving and caring; fair dealing, also, and restoration to a proper dignity and a true humanity were the gifts which he generously bestowed.

Sympathy and fellow-feeling have the kind of solidarity found in that notable chapter of St Matthew's gospel with its compassionate closing sentence, 'Inasmuch as you did it to one of the least of these brothers of mine, you did it to me.' It is significant that the scribes and artists of the Book of Kells, out of their life of community inspired by Colmcille, were moved to give special decoration to this practical expression of compassion for the hungry, naked, captive and thirsty of the world.

Part of such practical and positive sympathy for others is the empathy which compels us, through the right judgment of conscience, to put ourselves in the scenes and circumstances of those who accompanied Jesus on the way to the Cross, in order that we may think more clearly of what he does in and through us, in spite of our inadequacies and frequent lack of awareness.

'I sometimes think about the Cross': so runs a hymn greatly loved for the simplicity which takes the singer's thoughts to the heart of Christian truth.

There is an event confronting us. What happened at the trial and death of Jesus causes his friends and followers furiously to think. 'The cruel nails, the crown of thorns, and Jesus crucified for me.' The event, when thought about, concerns each Christian. The suffering and the agony hardly bear thinking about, we might timidly and tentatively say. Yet the Christian, signed with the sign of the Cross in baptism, is by definition a member of Christ, pledged not to be ashamed to confess the faith of the crucfied.

Thinking about the Cross makes demands of the heart. Only through thinking about the significance of the crucifixion is it possible to reach the heart of the matter. Here is the meaning of love. Here, too, the way of forgiveness. Furthermore, for those who see through the wounds to the healing, and through the death to the victory, the way of the Cross is discovered to be the way of light.

Thomas à Kempis puts it in words that have helped those not afraid to think and act sacrificially: 'if you carry your Cross willingly, it will carry you.' The finality of the Cross is the beginning of new life, fresh thinking. This is why the death of Jesus did not cause, for the faithful who witnessed the sequel, any second thoughts about their Master's power and promises; they thought and reasoned as he opened the Scriptures; doubts were dispelled, worries were turned into challenges, hesitations led to new visions, new thoughts.

Quiet Thought

An early prayer of the Christian Church seeks for help to serve God 'with a quiet mind'. It is a prayer that asks for pardon and peace; when these are granted the mind is at rest, and all that has disturbed it has been dealt with by God's reconciling power and generous forgiveness.

Quiet and rest and relaxation of the nerves and emotions go together in the spiritual life. Jesus himself sought quiet. He invited his companions to rest awhile, away from the milling crowds, who were coming and going. It was his custom to withdraw to a place apart, to climb a mountain, or to escape into the desert. Yet, wherever he found himself, either alone or with company, he revealed a strong quietude. This peace of mind was a positive spiritual resource. It gave him a calm control in the midst of troubles.

The mind and heart of Jesus were studied by the active, often agitated spirit of St Paul, in the midst of conflicts and much suffering. 'Have this mind among yourselves which you have in Christ Jesus,' he wrote to his beloved Philippians, 'who though he was in the form of God, did not count equality with God a thing to be grasped, but emptied himself, taking the form of a servant, being born in the likeness of men. And being found in human form he humbled himself and became obedient unto death, even death on a cross.' This famous meditation became woven into the thinking and worship of Christians. It is not surprising that the restless spirit of the writer discovered the secrets of inner peace the hard way; and was able to declare 'I have learned, in whatever state I am, to be content.'

The courageous Stephen also finds a peace which surpasses understanding, as the stones fly and the grinding teeth of his enemies gnash with fury. 'Lord Jesus, receive my spirit' had all the calmness of one whose mind was fixed on his master, because he trusted him to the uttermost. The words of prayer for his enemies also quelled the storm, 'Lord, do not hold this sin against them.' We perceive that in pardoning we are pardoned. Those, who are sorry for the murderers that kill and wound have caught the martyr spirit, free from bitterness and hate, and bear eloquent witness to the triumph of Christ over all divisions and conflicts. Such love and suffering in the life and death of the first martyr did not escape the notice or conscience of the young man called Saul who was there at the time, consenting to Stephen's death. This martyrdom stirred seed-thoughts in his mind.

Many a martyr has been a silent witness and a willing sufferer. Acceptance of conditions of life, as they were experienced, became a positive and powerful attitude, when situations that could not be changed were bravely endured. Christians were urged, on occasions, to study how to be quiet.

This quietness, this resting awhile, was encouraged by Jesus: In this way, his pupils learned that *to be* was more important than *to do*. Recreation renewed the mind and restored the spirit. So far from the somewhat sentimental picture of a gentle Jesus, 'meek and mild', as one of the later hymns suggests, there is a stronger portrayal of our Lord to be found in the quietness and confidence of his presence. The teaching of the gospels gives generous attention to attitudes, manners, approaches, states of mind and spirit.

In fact, the Christian way of life cannot be fully framed by rules. Nor can commandments and statutes, helpful as they are in maintaining discipline and encouraging definiteness, satisfactorily foster the spiritual life, on their own. There is a mysterious blend of love and justice, of suffering and joy which requires poetry and artistry for its expression.

Anxieties

'Be not anxious,' Jesus had said. He may have meant 'Do not keep worrying, but rather build up trustfulness, quietly and confidently.'

'Take no thought,' at first sounds a rash piece of advice; yet on reflection, the words discourage fuss and failure of nerve.

Singleness of mind must be cultivated by those who would grow in wisdom and seek to develop their character. Restless hearts find their true rest in the wise creator who works through hearts and minds, which are open and generous, at the ready for a life of dedicated service.

The Jerusalem Bible gives a modern ring to the familiar 'Take no thought'. 'Not to worry' is its version of the Greek word which points to a divided mind. 'Not to worry' has a lighter touch, perhaps, with just the right measure of encouragement in this piece of counselling. The older 'Take no thought' is completely misunderstood in our day. 'Be not anxious' perhaps overstresses the gloom and frustration in such a confused mental state.

Yet how do we banish the worry felt not only in violent and critical moments of danger and fear, but staying in the mind continually in a gnawing, nagging way. How can the directive 'Not to worry' bring any genuine comfort to those who have lost their employment, to the hungry and homeless whose needs are nothing short of agonising and desperate?

The advice 'Not to worry' occurs more than once in the recorded sayings of Jesus. In one place in the gospels, it follows the statement that no one can serve two masters. Worry has clearly its origin in divided loyalties and the experience of being torn apart by doubts and distractions. This way and that, inner thoughts whirl in confusion. The love-hate attitude of one who is the servant of two illustrates movingly the kind of contradictions and tensions which are all too familiar in our own waywardness and shilly-shallying. The single-minded have an overwhelming desire for 'one thing,' call it the vision of God or the love of truth. This single desire of the soul co-ordinates all that is fragmentary and falling apart in a distraught life.

'In nothing be anxious,' was also St Paul's recommendation, 'but in everything by prayer and supplication let your requests be made known to God. Let your moderation, or "sweet reasonableness" be made known to all.' He pointed to the power of prayer in overcoming the fears of the unknown.

Jesus also used the words 'be not anxious' when he observed a spirit of greed and possessiveness in those who were imprisoned by their riches and held in the grip of prosperity with all its attendant snares and burdens. He did not commend 'carelessness' or 'recklessness', but pointed rather to a sound stewardship of goods and a right use of the things which are available for our use. As has been said, 'Every disorder and calamity in life results from confusing the things we live by with the things we live for.' The divided loyalties of the mind will bring anxieties unless the search for the kingdom of God and his righteousness is made a priority.

The gospel's word for 'worry' is linked with a much stronger and more vigorously wounding word for what we might term 'fuss'. It occurs in the story of Martha who allows many things to confuse and trouble her. The loss of a sense of proportion and lack of concentration, in her case as in the experience of many another, lie at the root of much worry. Mary, on the other hand, had made a single choice and had found peace of mind. Yet the struggling eagerness of a Martha has an important contribution to make to the life of prayer.

The New Testament phrase for being of doubtful mind is in fact found also in the chatty, informal correspondence of the famous letters written on papyrus of the same period. These were unearthed from the sands of Egypt by archaeologists at the beginning of this century and introduced us to the ordinary everyday life of homes and families and also the commercial affairs of the market-place. A mother would conclude her letter to her son, away from home, with news of the family and a parting phrase: 'all well here; not to worry.'

We should also be more ready to share the worries of others, not by multiplying their worries, but by showing concern in order to lighten their loneliness and the burden of their perplexities. In assuming a corporate responsibility for the panic and the tears of things in our world, we avoid assigning the censure and blame, too readily heaped upon the unfortunate and the troubled. No Jack or Jill in any community is so much 'all right' that the plight of others, the wrong and the wronged, should not be thought of.

While it may be right 'not to worry' when hunger hits, jobs fail, and unhappy divisions disrupt, it is imperative that all should care, and turn the faithless mood of worry into loving concern and shared responsibility. If the poet was cryptic, he also perceived the dilemma when he wrote:

> Teach us to care and not to care
> Teach us to still.

Time to Think

'Be still my soul.' The prayer is a prelude for quiet thought. Only in the stillness, in the relaxed intervals, have we opportunity for thoughtful prayer. Lent is purposely lengthy in order that there may be time for prayers to mature and our thoughts to deepen.

In days of noise and rush, we may need to 'buy time', as the saying goes, if we are to practise some consecutive thinking. There is virtue in hastening slowly, when we read the Scriptures and when we pray our prayers enriched by the thoughts stirred through the reading.

To be able to relax in God's presence is to experience something of this maturing and development. Trains of thought are set in motion; ideas crystallise; imagination comes into play.

It takes time for self-consciousness to fade out, for love to cast out fears, and for words to give place to listening. We find ourselves, gradually and with time, at home in the presence of God. The opportunity is there to be still and rest.

'We have no power of ourselves to help ourselves.' If we think, we will depend more often on God. There is maturity in the recognition of our helplessness. There is no longer any need to be on the defensive. There is no point in advancing any self-justification. Trust takes the place of diffidence and awkward manners. Listening calls a halt to our nervous prattle and our formal patter.

There are times of course, in our uncertain lives, for cries from the heart, that are panic-stricken and despairing: 'O Lord, arise, help us,' we ejaculate. Emergencies have a way of creating faith; suffering creates sympathy and loving care in many a human predicament.

There is not, however, invariably the need to do 'something religious' when danger strikes and first aid is demanded. Crisis can cripple our hearts and stun our minds; we find that we cannot think; yet we can be aware that God has not withdrawn his protection, even when we are unable to communicate our love for him.

The Holy Spirit supplies what should be done and said, if

we are still ready to listen, to hold on, to be patient and receptive.

So we learn to persevere in prayer. The first steps in disciplining our thoughts undoubtedly count. Yet it is the continuity of the course of prayer, not the beginning only which 'yields the true glory'.

The notorious lady in the Betjeman poem was well-intentioned, but clearly immature. As she knelt in the Abbey at her prayers, with the throb of London's traffic outside, her thoughts revolved round her own feelings and preoccupations, as she went through the motions of praying for peace in the days of world war. How like her we are in our self-regard and impatient approach, when attempting to pray and marshal our thoughts and desires. She had the honesty to conclude her intercession with a human touch of weakness perhaps, and yet with an intimacy in her approach to God, which we dare not despise; at least there was no hypocrisy in the laugh-line

> and now, dear Lord, I cannot wait
> because I have a luncheon date.

In other ways we, too, have no power of ourselves to help ourselves.

Other Thinkers

We need to find maturity in our relationships with others, and not only in our private life of devotion with God. Those who differ from us in culture and creed have much to teach us about the Spirit's power. We learn to think when sharing thoughts with teachers of prayer. We learn from companions in prayer who join in intercession, if we listen with a sympathetic ear and an open heart to a different point of view, coloured as it may be by a tradition and experience other than our own.

Prejudice can halt our thinking all too easily. A refusal to listen and a resistance to learning new methods of prayer will surely stunt our spirits and stifle that growth in grace we search for when we make more time for prayer.

A prison chaplain has written fascinatingly about prayer.

The author of *In Jail with Jesus,* the Franciscan Brother, David Jardine, ministering in Belfast among prisoners has observed that prayer was relaxing. This might seem to be a surprising remark from one whose experience has largely been drawn from scenes of distress and loneliness. Yet his thinking on this aspect of prayer sounded convincing and realistic when he discussed the subject in a radio talk for many outside the gaol walls to hear.

Those who find it hard to make headway in the life of prayer and to put thought into this spiritual exercise, associate the worship of God with strenuous effort and the dull routine of discipline. They fail to find satisfaction because their efforts have been fruitless and the rules of prayer seemed barren and thoroughly strange.

It must be admitted that, whether in prison or out of it, it is difficult to have an air of naturalness in our praying. We shy off the traditional words; we are tense, certainly not relaxed, when there are pauses. We dread the silences and disturb them with our shuffling, both physical and mental. We do not perceive that there can be pools of silence to refresh a parched spirit; they can be used 'for a well' to cool us in our moments of impatience and resentment.

Often these feelings of grievance and self-pity enter in to block our thinking and ruin the prayer begun in good faith. The desire to start again vanishes. All is sterile in the desert of our minds.

At such a moment, it would appear to be quite out of the question that prayer could be relaxing. Yet teachers of prayer have had encouraging experiences, even in the most adverse circumstances, to pass on to those who are looking for a new approach to prayer.

Many who write on the subject emphasise that prayer can be enjoyed. In such enjoyment, relaxation is found and prayer is answered in terms of peace and the coming to terms with one's surroundings. There is a healing of the spirit, when 'calm of mind, all passion spent'.

Just as in the world of strains and pressures, there are many to be found who enjoy their work and the responsibilities that go with it, so in a steady life of faith and worship, the key to spiritual health and happiness may be found in the express enjoyment of discipline in prayer and the good habit of it which trains those who accept it in the art of concentration.

Once the breakthrough to enjoyment has been made, then is relaxation to be found. Masters of the devotional life speak of their delight in worship. They find that rejoicing and gladness of heart, added to their thankfulness, are quite in harmony with reverence and seriousness. They enjoy the work of prayer and it relaxes them. They testify to the truth of the famous answer at the beginning of the Shorter Catechism of the Church of Scotland about the chief end of man: 'the chief end of man is to glorify God and enjoy him for ever.'

There is a certain artistry in this 'resting in the Lord' with the experience of open-heartedness, calm, and, serenity. Did not a poet tell us out of scenes of bitter violence that 'the end of art is peace'? Behind the enjoyment, there lies an orderliness combined with a strong and sustained wish to trust in God wholly, and to find, for all our restlessness and sense of insecurity, that rest in him which brings out of spiritual agony the true ecstasy.

Holidays, away from work and the routine of domestic life, provide spiritual opportunities for those who have time off to absorb the beauty of the world about us. For a change, time can then be found to hear the sounds of the countryside, to allow the eyes to linger on the view of sea and sky, to drink in the stillness and peace of the landscape. The transition from such meditations upon the beauty of nature and the vastness of creation to a contemplation of God, his goodness and love, is made with surprisingly little effort, and enjoyed.

Such relaxation comes also in corporate worship, if we are sensitive to the welcoming friendliness of groups whose members are clearly 'of one mind, in one place.' When gathered for silence together, a leader of prayer can guide the assembled company from the first effort to observe a time of silence, with the familiar rustling, shuffling, and somewhat self-conscious unease, to a second and much deeper silence. Here God enters their thinking; they forget their surroundings and become part of a new unity in which others are thought of in terms of 'us' and no longer as 'them'. The worshippers, wrapt in silent thought, are loosed from all sorts of mental and spiritual prisons, and let go.

Ecumenical Thinking

In recent years, much prayer has been devoted to the improvement of inter-church relationships. Historical and doctrinal differences have been studied together in a new spirit of charity and understanding. Many denominational barriers have been removed by such efforts to worship and discuss the faith together. The week of Prayer for Christian Unity each January has enabled those not in communion with one another to find common ground, without ignoring sincerely held, if differing, convictions.

This regular consideration of 'our unhappy divisions' each year has done much for community life in Ireland. Neighbourliness of a new kind has been fostered in many areas, where there had been few contacts and a marked ignorance about the varying Christian traditions and practices.

Disunity has been recognised as something contrary to God's will. The words of Jesus in the high-priestly prayer of St John's seventeenth chapter include his longing that 'all may be one'. Penitence and the desire to change attitudes of mind and heart must be in the prayers of those who seek to be forgiven for sins and prejudice and intolerance. Increasingly, we need to be aware of our sharing of 'the one Christ' who is not divided.

We pray that God may be in our debating and discussion, in order that there may be honesty in our study of our heritage. This openness is part of ecumenical thinking. Through prayer it becomes possible, beyond our expectations, for disagreement to be accepted and understood without rancour or bitterness. To disagree without being disagreeable is the Christian approach in the search for ultimate unity. However far off the goal may appear to be, it is always necessary to pray with the vision of the one Christ before us, and to ask for patience and generous thinking in all our deliberations. The prayer of Reinhold Niebuhr has rescued many an encounter from frustration and hopelessness: the words have filled the ecumenical scene for many decades of this century:

> Grant me, Lord, the serenity to accept the things I cannot change;
> the courage to change the things that should be changed;
> and the wisdom to know the difference.

Controversy has created new thinking. Increasingly, it has been seen that the spirit of strife and hatred must have no place in Christian life. Often there will be disagreement among the interpreters of the faith. The prophets who explain the past and speak for the present, with an eye on their hopes for the future, do not all think alike. The ancient guide-line is worth remembering, as we ask that there may be 'unity, in essentials; liberty in unresolved, disputable matters; and in everything, charity'.

Ecumenical prayer emphasises the need for positive thinking and action. Churches should not pray against each other. Nor should prayer be judgmental. Many cultures, many languages, and many varying standards of living bring a warm humanity to prayers for a world in need of reconciliation.

All will find progress in mutual understanding if constant reference is made to God and our prayers ask that God be our judge. Let his Holy Spirit grant us the right judgment in all things, we are wise to pray. In our thinking, we ask that God's love and wisdom and justice may provide the criteria, as we weigh and debate the vexed questions that constantly recur in the history of the Church.

Non-theological factors, such as events in political life or disputes over territory and jurisdiction, may bedevil discussion, yet the search for the truth must be the dominating intent if thinking together is to be fruitful. We ask God in all these matters to take our minds and think through them.

In Ireland where history reveals the tangle that has intertwined religious and political issues, there have been courageous efforts by the differing Churches, through their leaders and their representatives, to re-examine some of the inherited, fixed positions. The desire to state in new terms the timeless truths of the faith makes exacting demands upon the intellect. A restatement of a cherished belief can stir emotions and blind the eyes to the main points in the arguments.

We ask that God may be in our thinking on such occasions to build up trust among the Churches, to plant fresh seeds of understanding, to point to areas of common action, that we may be open to change, and ready for the kind of compromise which combines apparently opposing views, without betraying convictions.

From that Irish venture in inter-church dialogue now known as 'Ballymascanlon' have emerged new lines of thought. Cooperation in biblical study has helped the different traditions to find common ground. Parallel statements on doctrines concerning biblical authority and ways of worship, as well as varied disciplines in the field of morals, have stimulated fresh thinking.

It has become possible for any Church, stating its position, to ask of another Church what is its teaching on this subject, what is the distinctive element which causes the difference of opinion and belief. How crucial is this? Or is this a difference rather than a distinction? So the questions multiply and the discussion develops.

These conferences, begun in 1973 at Ballymascanlon Hotel, near Dundalk in Ireland, have done much to encourage frankness, sincerity, and honesty among the Churches. The personal contact made between accredited representatives of the member Churches of the Irish Council of Churches and the Roman Catholic hierarchy has been widely welcomed. Even if many problems remain unsolved, the new approach has had a spiritual influence of great significance, both inside and outside Ireland. Separated Christians have met and made plans for continued meetings, in order that they may learn together in faith and obedience what is God's will for their future.

Thinking is what we pray for, human thinking guided by the goodness and the wisdom of God. Popular slogans have been found misleading and too simplistic. Formulae, drawn up at a particular period of Christian history, carry in their phrasing and tone much of the confessional issues of the past period, when a definition was deemed necessary. Words, inevitably limited for the task of expressing eternal truths, deserve analysis and re-consideration. No one can afford to stop thinking about the words of faith and life, least of all the representatives who work and speak on behalf of their fellow-members.

More than one Church has expressed the need for a think-tank of trained and experienced Christian leaders of thought and action in order that the written statements of varying authority from the past should not lose their life and become dead letters of academic and historic interest only. Thinking before we speak, readiness to hear the other side before we make decisions, thinking with humility and courage at the same time; these are demands made upon the Churches, not merely for the defence of the faith in a time of great opposition from outside Church life, and not a little apathy, but more profitably for a clearer, more thrustful, declaration of belief.

In some respects, the Irish School of Ecumenics earns the description of a think-tank, although in fact its activities are much wider, extending to all the subjects touched upon by academic theology, as well as interpreting the signs of the times in Christianity today, for the benefit of improving inter-church relationships.

In Ireland, there is in many places a friendly feeling about ecumenism, once the word is fully understood. Where it is looked upon with suspicion and even with fear and active hostility, regrettably little effort is made to understand its scope or its limitations. Needless to say, ecumenism does not refer to the seeking of Christian unity at any price, nor does it commend the absorption of many traditions by one tradition in any forcefully authoritarian manner.

The subject demands thoughtful prayer. Ecumenism does in fact stir people, when they meet and talk together about the things of God, to think afresh over what had not occurred to them in quite the same way when alone or confined to their own confession. Faith has a way of becoming more positive and committing when believers find that they must be more articulate in the presence of other sorts of Christians. It is quite usual to find many from various sections of society who have not ventured to speak about their beliefs in adult terms, or in words which reveal that they have been thinking out spiritual matters for themselves.

In the field of ecumenical activity, there is more than mere camaraderie and courtesy, important as these personal qualities are. The 'school', now ten years old, has shown through its curriculum how essential it is for proper understanding and the strengthening of mutual trust that there should be a serious study of the causes behind the present disunity. There should also be some shared practical projects in the disciplines of the Churches, their pastoral methods, and the distinctive contributions from the several denominations. Good relationships create good human beings, it has been said.

The recent marking of the first decade in the life of this 'school', founded with the motto 'floreat ut pereat', 'may its work flourish in such a way that there will be no longer any need for it to exist; if its problems are solved, then it may go out of business'.

Its history to date has enabled attention to be drawn to the urgency of fostering a spirit of reconciliation and generous understanding among divided Christians in Ireland. In addition, students enrol from countries abroad with the same desire for improved relationships in the world Church as the word 'ecumenical' suitably implies.

In this procedure, ignorance and prejudice are replaced by honest discussion and frank criticisms. arguments if they are to be constructive require scholarly information and reliable evidence for their support. Unexpected and promising results emerge when fears are banished from the company in colloquy and a warm charity melts the cold reserve, and sacred subjects can be treated with a new sense of ease and a relaxed naturalness.

Furthermore, this kind of thinking together opens up opportunities for advancing the cause of human justice and world peace. Christians soon find common ground when help for the oppressed and relief for the hungry are seen to be spiritual priorities without question or controversy from any section of the ecumenicals assembled.

Jesus who brought peace where there was division also advanced the cause of peace by the offering of himself in the struggle and suffering which led to the perfect work of reconciliation he completed from the Cross.

Suffering and conflict in other parts of the world far from religious strife and controversy have alerted many Christians to be deeply penitent about that element in the complicated Irish scene which has religious roots. The corruption of the best has proverbially the worst results. The thoughtful find in their awareness of the sins of many generations including our own that the virtues of faith, hope, and love must be genuinely, impartially, and with a wide generosity applied to the whole of life, individual, social, and, to use the world-wide expression, ecumenical. Too often the three virtues that stem from God's grace and are filled with God's life have received lip-service from us. Faith, hope and love deserve constant and concentrated thought from the heart. We receive them, by God's help, that we may use them in all our life and work, dedicated to his praise and his glory.

Calling to Mind

Thinking is a sort of remembering. The Scriptures indicate that 'remember' is a word of many meanings. They reveal the important truth that remembering demands from us more than a feat of memory and a sharp alert brain. Remembering should be, and is often recognised to be, a spiritual exercise and a spiritual responsibility.

Thus the biblical word for 'remember' expresses thanksgiving. With the thinking and the thanking involved there is an acknowledgment of God's goodness in the past. Remembering spells encouragement for the present and inspiration for the future. If we think about this, and recall what we have been taught, there have been many good precedents to strengthen our faith in God's goodness and to find that we are not afraid to reason about God just as we are not ashamed to adore him.

The psalms in their praises, for example, call to mind the wonders and blessings of old times. An awareness of life's testing conditions is kindled by the recording and recounting of many deliverances and rescuings from dangers and disasters. The very thought of these draws forth gratitude and praise.

Remembering also warns. It teaches lessons and bids us see in perspective our present discontents. If we are doubtful that 'we have never had it so good', can we be any more sure in our depressions that 'the world since it began has never had it so bad'. 'Remember', in the biblical sense, sounds at times like a command, a directive, a bidding. Remember God's goodness, but also, to quote the old carol, 'Remember Adam's fall.'

Remember Zion with affection and longing, they were told, because it appeared disastrous to be cut off from all the benefits and resources of a spiritual centre for the nation. 'If I forget thee, O Jerusalem, let my right hand forget her cunning.'

Remembering was an essential for exiles in a far country, for captives fast forgetting the sweetnesses of freedom.

'Remember thy Creator' . . . 'Remember Lot's wife' . . . 'Remember to keep holy the Sabbath day' . . . so runs a chain of remembrances through the pages of the people's history. These lessons from the past shed light upon the problems of today's living.

Here are insights provided for us to help our good judgment and to supply us with guide-lines as we face parallel experiences, often of an unnerving kind in current world affairs.

A mood of remembrance makes us think of the good examples of saints and heroes who have contributed to the tradition we inherit. We stir our hearts and minds to think also of short, brave, ordinary lives whom we all too easily forget, remembering that their influences and contribution are known to God and form part of the unknown good which we freely enjoy.

Remembrance becomes productive and fulfilling when the ingredients of prayer, praise, thanksgiving, encouragement, experience, and ever deeper understanding of life's mysteries are accorded a place in the simplest offering of the heart and mind in love to God. We find our heart and mind united in the highest expression of this love when, at the breaking of bread and the taking of the cup we do as he commanded, in remembrance of him.

Chapter V

'God be at mine end,
And at my departing'

This prayer of life is open-ended. So should all prayer be. The words come to an end, but the grace and the meaning linger on.

These last verses sum up the human life. The end is not yet, and when death comes, all will not be over, for the end is a departing. There will be at the close of our earthly journey no dead end, but a way through and a voyage out.

This word 'end' claims our attention. We do well at every stage of life to look to the end. By doing so, we put ourselves in God's perspective, in his setting of eternity. In him is no end and no beginning.

In one sense, there is an end in every beginning which we make. Each new initiative of ours springs from what seems past and over; yet the new start carries forward much that in fact is not finished off. So complex is our life, influenced by history and tradition, yet only fully understood in the wider context of a life beyond.

Whatever happens to us, we discover that it is rarely possible to declare that, after our experience of any event, a chapter in our life has closed and all is over. The end of a world war was the beginning of new developments among the nations. The end of a personal quarrel can mean the reinforcing of an old friendship that had temporarily turned sour. A bereavement, deeply felt to be a cruel loss, bringing devastating loneliness, has been known to become strangely and mysteriously creative. A new start, after a much-loved companion has departed this life, brings a fresh vision of life's needs and opportunities to those that are left, with their faith not merely intact but, to their strange surprise, richly blossoming. Such sequels come for those who look back not in anger or bitterness, but in gratitude. After the break, and sudden sense of loss, they refuse to stay in the past, but bring the gifts of love and friendship, which they still treasure, into their planning of the next step ahead.

The end of life is the beginning of an adventure; it is not a blank void, but a fascinating mystery. Interruptions in life also remind us that the continuities which we count precious are not mere, monotonous repetitions of past years and former days, but unforeseen beginnings. There are few of us who cannot find some ring of truth in the thought that the poet T. S. Eliot put into his poem *East Coker,* 'In my beginning is my end.'

If we add to our thinking about death all that our faith in the risen Christ gives to us, then the word adventure becomes an appropriate description of 'our departing'. It suggests a new start into a wider, if unknown, life, with new conditions, undetailed and unspecified. Yet what is known about life with Christ already assures us that our spiritual journey of a lifetime is to be continued. Christ for the Christian is final; but he lives in this glorious finality; because he lives, we, that are Christ's, live also.

It is significant that we prepare for Christmas and the birth of Jesus, his entering into our world, and all that we associate with a new creation, by reflecting during the season of Advent on what are called the last things.

In this dramatic way, the end and the beginning are held together. The meaning of Christmas is only fully disclosed at the end of the life of Jesus, not at the beginning. Although, of course, there had been prophecies and expectations about the birth of Christ, it was only after his death that people began to think about the origins of this babe that was born. Christmas was not the first Christian festival to be celebrated by the Church; Easter was the first festival to be celebrated, and in the light of resurrection the earlier events in the life of the risen Lord were interpreted and more fully understood.

Accordingly in the weeks before the birthday of Christ is observed, the last things at the other end of life are called to mind. Death and judgment and 'in the end, God' have all assumed a new look since the Word became flesh.

The German custom of lighting candles as the days of Advent progress to flood the Advent wreath with light in the homes and churches of the people picturesquely symbolises our thinking about our ultimate destiny. Death has been transformed since Christ died; 'by his death, he destroyed death,' its chill and lonelinees have been replaced by his welcoming presence. Judgment is no longer to be faced apart from his love and mercy.

The seasons, as they come round, repeat the themes of faith through fast and festival. Each year finds us harking back to beginnings and endings with a different approach as our moods change. We who are changeable and in regular need of the penitence, which means a change of heart, find to our comfort that in the end the facts of our faith have been constant and changeless.

The exploration of these mysteries becomes a lively concern. Each round of preparation and celebration can take us deeper and further into the ocean of endless life and love. We are privileged to share these gifts which God bestows continually. Kept as it were in eternal life, through prayer and worship, by word and sacrament, we are given strength to pass through things temporal. Only with God's end in view can we see ourselves clearly, not in the clutch of the circumstances and pressures of the world, but in God's hands.

There are all sorts of loose ends in our lives. We need spiritual help to rescue them and to tie them into the pattern provided by this prayer which shapes our actions. The frayed ends of good intentions unsustained, of distractions uncontrolled, of idle follies, the envies, hatred and maliciousness listed with many another disorder in the litanies of penitence, are innumerable and notorious.

These imperfections, which spoil the character and damage the person, demand spiritual attention. If the phrase 'Be perfect' has the generally accepted interpretation, 'be fitted, or orientated, to a life of true and complete fulfilment,' then the sins of commission and omission that leave us imperfect may well be termed 'loose'. If what is perfect is consistent with the true and good end of life, the imperfect fails to further that aim. Sin breaks the connection with God; many sins have varied aims, motives and ends which defy and even deny God, his law, and his love.

The Christian is wise to keep the true end in view at every stage of life. A young person from early days of speaking and praying can include with sincerity and realism this closing petition, 'God be at mine end.'

To use those words and to appreciate that in our way of speaking 'there is no end,' requires more mature thought than can be expected in our earliest years. So we think of 'end' as 'fulfilment' or 'perfection'. At the same time, at our best, we know we fall short of God's glory; we will never exhaust the possibilities of this prayer for God to be at our end. Our chief concern is to be with God in all that happens; we are not to worry about what we have achieved. If no goal is reached and no race finished, we need not feel the hopelessness of frustration, for faith is there to make much of little. Faith discloses to us the joy of being in the presence of God, the end of our faith, which is the salvation of our souls. As Catherine of Siena put it, 'God does not ask a perfect work, but infinite desire.'

This sense of the end is frequently found in the prayers of the Church. The service of Compline presents in its shape and structure a picture of our life in the context of its end. So far from being an obsolete or archaic piece of devotion from the early centuries, marked as they were by persecution and the short lives of martyrs, Compline has retained its popular appeal. Its name indicates completion. Its daily use encourages us to take one day at a time, to live in the present with all its dangers and uncertainties, and even to 'live this day as if our last'.

The popular Epilogue, occupying but a few moments of radio time, often has echoes of this office of Compline which originated in a monastic atmosphere, but now has an acknowledged significance for those who seek to end the day in the informality of home or in the open air round the camp-fire on a summer evening. Here are words of trust and dependence, as the sun sets, and the lights are going out and the day is done. The whole of life, its work, its enjoyment, and its demands are summed up and dedicated to God.

The hymn at the hour of Compline begins with the words, 'Before the ending of the day,' and yet in some way we know that our day never ends. We are conscious, however, that each day, as it draws to a close, demands of us some review and a summing up. We bring to a pause what we have attempted during our waking hours, and trust that God will continue in us without even our conscious cooperation what through his grace has begun in our lives. We remember that it is he who 'has made us and not we ourselves'. In one day's activities with all its petty experiences, the details and the duties of routine, we try to see significance. If, while achievements are small, attitudes to others and the spirit of the work have not spoiled the day, then a sense of completion and fulfilment can be found, even in the short term of a day. What has been done, imperfect and unfinished as it usually is, will be properly placed in God's hands. We ask him at one and the same time to forgive us and to bless us for the effort. The end of the day is an end of a special kind, for it is 'to be continued'. The day's thought and the day's work form an episode in the life of the Christian. The day closes with an epilogue rather than a conclusion.

The four psalms selected for recital at Compline help us to 'look to the end'. They carry a message of peace, trust, faith, and praise, four continuing gifts from God who 'preserves us, while waking, and guards us while sleeping'.

The first of these psalms (Psalm 4) presents a picture of an anxious farmer, concerned about the possible invasion of his land by a destructive enemy. He fears for the harvest of corn, wine and oil, and he has no ordinary means of protecting the crops; disaster faces him and would have resulted in total despair, if he had not God to turn to. In the midst of this personal and material loss. God is seen as the farmer's defence against the foe. The light of leadership that God shows in the darkness that overshadows the scene transforms the worry and depression into peace of mind. The psalm is a kind of dialogue; the farmer's conversation reveals his questionings and perplexities. When the reassuring answers come and promise well, then a spiritual harvest, a hidden and profitable asset, counteracts the fear of famine and waste. The calm, closing words at the end of the farmer's day, have been on the lips of many another in sickness or anxiety: 'I will lay me down in peace and take my rest; for it is thou, Lord, only that maketh me dwell in safety.' This peaceful conclusion prepares us for another day, with sleep to refresh the body and the mind. The spirit of peace allows the grace of God to work upon our nature.

The second of the Compline psalms (Psalm 31, verses 1-6) reminds us that this late evening service is linked with a particular moment in the life of Jesus Christ. In it occur the words 'Into thy hands I commend my spirit,' familiar to all who know the narrative of the Crucifixion, as told by St Luke. At the end of the day, we recall that Jesus rested in the sepulchre after his death on the Cross. His last words have become famous. They also have much to teach us about death and our approach to death. He suffered more than we can imagine. In mind, body and spirit, he endured the pain which is called bluntly and realistically without any sentimentality 'agony and bloody sweat'. Yet his trust in God never failed; he felt all the deep suffering that the experience of loneliness and forsakenness can bring; but at the end, he entrusted himself to the Father to whom he prayed, into whose hands he committed himself. He also cried 'It is finished' with a note of victory in the phrase which surely meant that his work was accomplished. This kind of finishing did not imply that all was over, but rather the work achieved brought blessed results to the world for the future. The psalm puts words into the mouth of those who sing or say it in order to increase their trust through Christ in God. At the end of the day, at the end of life, at the end of a war or a crisis, they can bear repeating for they wear well. They keep fresh in our minds the story of our redemption. 'Into thy hands, O Lord, I commend my spirit; for thou has redeemed me, O Lord, thou God of truth.'

Psalm 91, the third of the Compline psalms, strengthens the faith of the fearful. Those who dread the dark are challenged to put their trust in God who rules the night as well as the day. As another psalm emphasises, the darkness is no darkness with God. That there are dangers and risks in the darkness, Psalm 91 makes clear. This was a memorable psalm in the days of the Second World War with the repeated bomb attacks on the cities. One watchman, on duty to raise the alarm and to urge the people to find what shelter and protection might be available, recalled the poignant words of this psalm as he kept vigil. 'Thou shalt not be afraid for any terror by night . . . a thousand shall fall beside thee, and ten thousand at thy right hand, but it shall not come nigh thee.' The old words that promised protection to those who put their trust in God, come what may, brought timely courage and built up a faith that was being grimly tested.

The fourth and last in the series, Psalm 134, was associated with the pilgrimage made to the Temple. At night the pilgrims came to their journey's end and a meeting with their Lord. Praise and thanksgiving were offered at the culmination of their spiritual effort. Compline sometimes has seemed 'a sad hour' with tasks unfinished and fears unidentified, but there is always a place 'at the end' for giving thanks or praise to the God whose love never comes to an end. Some have connected this pilgrim-song with the return of exiles from captivity, after a long absence from the spiritual centre in the great city. For them, the end of their journey was like a new beginning. Others in our day have had similar experiences, as the poet Eliot has beautifully expressed it:

> We shall not cease from our exploration
> And the end of all our exploring
> Will be to arrive where we started
> And know the place for the first time.

The vigilance of Compline enriches the practice of prayer. The darkness shuts out wandering and distracted thoughts. The watchers by night have an alertness not easily found in the afternoon. There is discipline in keeping watch; guarding tongue and eyes is an exacting spiritual exercise. Correspondingly, we are grateful to God for watching over us in the night; 'Guard us waking,' we pray, 'guard us sleeping; and when we die' recalling Richard Whately's verse, set to the tune of 'All through the night'.

At the end of the day, we are kept 'as the apple of an eye'. This picture of the eye tells us much about the protecting love of God which surrounds us and continues actively to keep us safe without any initiatives or efforts on our part. The 'apple' or pupil of the eye is closely garrisoned by lid and lash. Any foreign body that comes upon it from outside to startle or damage meets with a speedy reflex action. The response of muscle to cover and protect is instant. So God bestows his grace that anticipates our felt needs; he knows 'our necessities before we ask, and our ignorance in asking'.

Compline has kept the song we know as Nunc Dimittis in circulation, popularising in a good sense the incident in the Temple at Jerusalem when the old man Simeon took the young child Jesus in his arms. 'Now lettest thou thy servant depart in peace,' was the old man's prayer at the end of a long life. He had had a long wait, also. This end of the road for him was a climax. His was a joyful and trustful response to exceptionally good news. The 'now' that introduces the song represents more than perfect timing; it brought this ancient servant of God face to face with life eternal. All his expectations were summed up in the tiny life of a saviour and deliverer.

Simeon, in his role of prophet, declared that this child, coming at a moment of crisis, was 'set for the rise and fall of many'. In the end, Christ will supply the answers to many questions; his judgments will prevail. He will triumph over all our sins and divisions. There will be a 'last day' when he will come again to judge both living and dead. Crisis has the note of judgment at its root.

At the end of the day, at the end of an era, the words of the song hold out a permanent promise. The old man had had the courage and patience to wait. Patience on many occasions must precede our prayer 'God be at mine end, and at my departing.'

So when we sing Nunc Dimittis in the dusk at the hour of Compline, we picture the scene of that night. This last word at the end of a long and faithful life matches our mood at the close of a day's round of work and, perhaps, patient waiting. It marks a moment of trust and committal.

It is not difficult to appreciate why this song of light and glory is often heard at a funeral when there is a departing in peace. With the ending of this life, a new beginning already shines through the weaknesses and pain. Light and glory have been created in the dark places of suffering and struggle. In the end, life's true meaning has been disclosed and evil has been overcome with good.

'Departing in peace' meant much more than an ebbing of physical strength or a slipping away from this life unnoticed. The peace happily granted, and often prayed for, is strong and wholesome. It is possible to die well, with a dignity and an integrity, when our 'eyes have seen thy salvation'. There is an exceeding weight of glory in this concept of peace. Where Christ is, there is salvation.

'Lighten our darkness' is a key-prayer in our close of day worship. It reflects the work and calling of Jesus. As the Light of the world, he shone in the darkness and was not overwhelmed by it.

In fact, the darkness at times dazzled. Light shone in the darkness and made clear much that was mysterious and murky. Light itself can be blinding, while the mystery of darkness may illuminate some deep, human problems. The Christian gospel, for example, is made strangely clear when the blind evidently perceive what others, with physical sight unimpaired, fail to observe.

Jesus, ever compassionate, may have been more concerned to bring light to the insensitive, the obtuse, and the blind of heart than to concentrate on the healing of the physically disabled. In any case, the blind Bartimaeus and the other blind man in the gospels have helped many to see the invisible. Seeing may not have been believing; believing, however, clearly brought a new sight, a second sight. On a famous occasion, it was declared to be a positive blessing not to see, and yet to believe.

There was darkness at the crucifixion. 'Darkness was over the whole land,' we read. Paradoxically, the light of the cross relieved the gloom. The way of the cross was perceived to be a way of light, as many an artist has sought to portray.

There was darkness, too, in the hearts of those who

betrayed and denied Jesus. the one 'in whom was light' reveals for us the blackness of despair and the eclipsing effect of spiritual failure. Judas went out of the lighted supper-room and it was night. After the dull thud of Peter's words of denial, the Lord turned and looked on him and the 'eye of his lord lightened his darkness'.

We learn to see the light when we grope our way through the dark tunnel and discover that we are nearly at the other end. 'The dark night of the soul' precedes illumination. Many kinds of darkness, sorrows, despairs, and shames shut out the light. Yet they also provide experiences that teach us valuable truths. We learn the hard way and find ourselves enlightened, wiser, and more spiritually mature, as a result. Many, like Nicodemus, have felt protected by the darkness as they searched for the light they failed at first to see. For such, the dark is light enough.

Departure

'Departing in peace', to quote the phrase from the Nunc Dimittis, in one sense appeared to mark the exit of Simeon who represented the old order, so that a way might be made clear for the Messiah.

Yet, on reflection, we see in this departure not an exit but an 'exodus', a way through, a journey on. What is part of earlier history has not been rejected nor ignored; there is rather a fulfilment of prophecy and promise. A renewal of creation is announced. Those who are 'in Christ' became new creatures.

This glorious hope expressed by the word 'departing' in our prayer brings a reminder of the scene on the mountain of Transfiguration, when Jesus stood out alone, as a unique figure, in a glorious light. Not only was he transfigured, but after his death, the character of death was transformed and altered for all who believed in him. 'To be with Christ' was far better.

The Transfiguration could scarcely be understood apart from the history of the Old Testament. When Jesus spoke of his 'decease' which he should 'accomplish' at Jerusalem, we perceive that these words and phrases are loaded with meanings, coloured by the significant historical events which the people of Israel constantly and thankfully recalled.

'Decease' described not only a death, but a death with a purpose. This death was transformed into one of the joyful mysteries of life, wonderfully discovered by faith and revealed to the world. The 'exodus' of Jesus was a deliverance. He brought people out of darkness into his light. He freed them from the slavery in which sin imprisons human life, and brought the liberty and new life which forgiveness bestows. There were difficulties and disciplines on this journey through a wilderness beset with temptations and in the midst of opposition that ended in the offering of his life by crucifixion, the supreme sacrifice. All that was meant by this exodus was found in the life and death of Jesus only. He was unique. The sacredness of life and the importance of the individual were affirmed.

The historical Exodus from Egypt under the leadership of Moses provided an everlasting theme of redemption, rescue, liberation, and eternal life. The people, who were brought out of the darkness and slavery under a foreign rule, found a new life after many trials and sufferings, in a promised land, where what had been mere existence was transformed into responsible living.

At the end of the Christian story of salvation brought through Jesus, there is a summing up made by the evangelists, who compiled the record and reported the events. History, teaching, interpretation, and worship combine to present what was seen and heard.

The prophecies about Jesus, the annunciation of his birth, his nativity, passion, death, resurrection, and ascension have all revealed God's glory and the truth about the life he gives. Through these events, we come to know God and ourselves. 'This is life eternal,' to quote the words of the prayer of Jesus, in the seventeenth chapter of St John's gospel, 'that they know thee the only true God, and Jesus Christ whom thou hast sent.'

The kind of God, to whom we look 'at our end' is seen and adored in family terms. Father, Son, and Spirit signify fellowship and love. The marks of suffering and compassion shine through this relationship. The wonder of it all can be discovered in the glory of human heroism and a generous love that gives 'but does not count the cost'. Heaven and earth were enfolded in a single peace when the Word was made flesh.

It is often fascinating to study the last words uttered by those who are at the point of death. Some last words have appeared particularly trivial or banal; others have a prophetic touch; they seem to sum up a whole philosophy of life in a phrase, or reveal a faith hitherto concealed, or betray a dominant characteristic 'at the moment of parting'.

In a similar way, the final sentences of each of the four gospels of the New Testament make a fascinating study. Each evangelist, whether Matthew, Mark, Luke or John records in a distinctive way the end of all that Jesus began to do and to teach.

In each case, as might be expected, the end has a sequel. St Matthew's 'Go and make disciples of all nations' has proved prophetic. Written at first, with a measure of hind-sight, the great fact of Christian history in our era has caused many to be astounded at the world-wide scale of the gospel's proclamation. The directive, however, remains. The word which has gone out 'to the ends of the earth' has to be received – and repeated. At every end, as the goal of each missionary enterprise is reached, there is a cry for new beginnings. The Church's mission, which began from Jerusalem, now finds inspiration and fresh impetus from countries far away from the early scenes of the preaching and teaching of the gospel. New light on the old faith shines from the pages of missionary history in every continent.

Saints and martyrs are still being made; where there is poverty, violence, injustice and distress, disciples of Christ have been found faithful and effective, sustained by the knowledge that he is with them always, 'to the close of the age', to quote St Matthew's last phrase.

The end of St Mark has in some manuscripts left us with an abrupt and somewhat daunting account of one resurrection experience, 'They said nothing to anyone, for they were afraid.'

Other manuscripts take us further and add that the faithful 'preached everywhere; while the Lord worked with them and confirmed the message with signs following'.

That 'signs did follow' the resurrection we are all assured. St Mark's last words in his gospel's 'longer ending' help us to interpret 'the end' in terms of 'results'. Things began to happen when all seemed to be over. The first sense of abruptness caused by shock and terror was replaced by a burning zeal to share the experience with the world.

The two alternative endings of Mark provide us with a blend of joy and woe, a common enough human experience which most of us are called upon to taste.

St Mark's gospel is told dramatically. Event follows event and the reader is caught up into the action. For the outsider, these events may remain mere happenings; for the believer, they become experiences, many of them disturbing and revolutionary; they invite further action.

Our prayer 'God be at mine end' helps us in the terror and astonishment shared understandably by all who find themselves on the brink of a great discovery. The mystery of death is both awesome and bewildering; the joy of the resurrection seemed, perhaps, too good to be true, too overwhelming to be entirely free from a sense of shock and fear.

'God be at mine end' thus is a timely prayer for those who are stunned at the thought of dying, feeling themselves trapped in a spiritual cul-de-sac, called to face the loneliness and isolation that accompany their experience.

St Luke, also, at the close of a gospel narrative written in a very different style, points to the continuity of all that had taken place. As has been said, the gospel never ends. 'They returned to Jerusalem with great joy,' he concludes, 'and were continually in the temple praising God.' Worship and praise of God was the highest form of dedicated service. Just so the Gloria of liturgical worship asserts the continuity of prayer and its eternal character in the oft-repeated words 'Glory be to the Father and to the Son and to the Holy Spirit, as it was in the beginning, is now, and ever shall be.' This does not indicate a reluctance for movement or change among the faithful, conscious of their tradition. Admittedly, the satirists and critics have had occasion to point to the words as examples of archaism and monotony in the Church's witness. On the contrary, they express unbroken, sustained life. If mention is made of 'the beginning,' there is no recommendation to return to the beginning in an attempt to set the clock back. Timelessness and eternity are to be found in the life of the Spirit at every period of history.

Those who praised God for the good news of the gospel followed up their worship with service out and beyond the city and the Temple. St Luke had compiled a second volume; in all probability the Acts of the Apostles were recorded by him as author and narrator. The sequel of the gospel was found, not in reflections, theories, or personal opinions but in facts of history, events which revealed the power of the risen Lord in people's lives to bring healing, to give them hope and vision. The Acts of the Apostles has sometimes been called the Gospel of the Holy Spirit, so clearly are the life and power of the Spirit to be seen in all that is recounted. The last of the Acts is also highly significant. The story is not over when the twenty-eighth chapter of this period of Church history comes to a close. The work went on 'unhindered'. The end is left open. That word 'unhindered' is packed with meaning; it suggests freedom, continuity, wider scope, further opportunity for a gospel that is everlasting.

The fourth gospel, that according to St John, supplements this thinking about the end and the beginning of our faith. He had written his unusual account with a special aim and a distinctive plan, in order that his readers might believe 'that Jesus is the Christ, the Son of God, and that believing you may have life in his name'. Then, informally, almost casually, he concludes: 'There are also many other things which Jesus did: were every one of them to be written, I suppose the world itself could not contain the books that would be written.'

This was St John's way of showing that not a book, or even a library of books, but only a life could express the love, the truth, and the holiness which were revealed. Christianity ultimately is Christ. And Christ himself is the final revelation.

These last words in the concluding paragraphs of the four gospels, all different in style and emphasis, yet at the same time consistent, encourage us to consider the Ascension and the departing of our Lord. Through him, risen, ascended, glorified, we learn about our departing.

'He was parted from them! The bald statement, the blunt description, records a deep experience. Artists and writers have subsequently brought colour to the scene and lent it majesty.

The Ascension guides our thoughts about the unseen and the eternal. Jesus departed in peace, but not before he had given his word of peace to those he was to leave. 'Peace I leave with you, my peace I give to you; not as the world gives, I give to you,' he had said. Peace at the last is what we pray for ourselves and for others as preparation is made for death. No longer limited by local conditions, the ascended Lord is made available everywhere, for everyone. No longer anchored as it were, the Ascension is a voyaging out and away beyond our horizons.

'He was parted from them.' The simple statement of St Luke is free from sensationalism. 'A distance' was set between the master and his disciples. Out of sight, he was still very much in their minds. The parting found them joyful not sorrowful. There was no sense of loss. This was no bereavement. They were already looking to the future. They had work to do.

In fact, they had a sense of fulfilment. The parting of friends created a new relationship. The new experience assured those who were left behind that they had a definite commission and a strong responsibility. The cloud that came between Jesus and the men of Galilee did not mystify them. A 'cloud', after all, in the idiom they knew, often denoted the presence of God. This farewell was clearly no ordinary kind of separation.

Thoughts about the Ascension concentrated upon the person of Christ rather than upon the place from which he departed. The heart of our belief in the Ascension lies in the continuing presence of Christ in a manner no longer limited, not even by the sky beyond the clouds. He is with us always, even to the end of the world.

His life, widely available, is not conditioned by any one particular culture or nationality. His humanity, now glorious and victorious, continues to reveal the love of God 'at all times, and in all places'. Jesus Christ is the same yesterday, today, and for ever.

An ordinary human life, such as ours, is remembered for a while. Then, gradually, the recollection of it by others grows dim. Most lives sink into oblivion. The few are remembered in history for their achievement. Famous men are praised; some have no memorial 'but their name liveth for evermore'.

When we pray that God should be with us at the end, we remember the ascended Lord who 'ever lives to make intercession' for us. The memory of Jesus was certainly not blotted out by his departing. His influence widened, his presence became more vivid, and his love for those whom we have forgotten, for the rejected, the uncared for and unloved, is limitless and overflowing.

We do not gaze up into the skies and ask where has Jesus gone. We think rather of what he does for us still. His living presence and his loving service are the cause of our joy and gratitude. There are countless ways in which we discover that he lives. The short affirmation sung, and sometimes shouted, in the worship of the Church are full of this spirit of thanksgiving: 'Christ has died, Christ is risen, Christ will come again.'

These succinct acclamations have a long history of faith behind them. There is a great cloud of witnesses to testify to the spiritual discoveries constantly made through their life with the living Lord, 'risen, ascended, glorified'.

It was probably not a surprise for us to learn from certain 'space-men' at the time of their return from that wonderful and breath-taking journey to the moon and back that they had found no angels in the heavens. Nor had they experienced any spiritual encounters which could not have been shared while on the earth's ground. The report, however, that they felt they had penetrated 'eternal silences' was moving and impressive. Those who ventured on these expeditions have added to our knowledge of creation and thus increased our sense of wonder. Père Teilhard de Chardin used to say, when conducting his researches in natural science, that the more deeply he studied creation, the more mysterious he found it, and the stronger became his belief in a faithful creator.

Explorers, scientists, and all kinds of serious searchers after truth, with heart and mind 'ascending', frequently admit that their humility increases as they progress in their work. The sense of personal pride, if any, which they feel in any achievement or experiment, becomes remarkably muted.

Our fears of the unknown have been reduced through the findings of the specialist whose explanations reveal causes and diagnose disorders and puzzling perplexities about ourselves and our surroundings. Our fears about a responsible use of the knowledge discovered and about the handling of creation would overwhelm us if the guidance and judgment of the faithful Creator were totally ignored and flouted in his world.

We speak in a casual way about 'our time'. We are inclined to think selfishly about conditions of life and policies, public or private, which will suffice 'for our time'. We also pray in a traditional way for peace 'in our time'.

It is well to remember that our times are in God's hands. There is, we know, a time to die – and to depart this life. The popular songs of the day reflect an acute awareness of the temporal and the temporary. The words of Ecclesiastes, chapter 4, have made a come-back: 'For everything there is a season and a time, for every matter under heaven; a time to be born and a time to die.' A recent pop song asks the question of the fans in the audience, and all who are listening in, 'What's another year?' This sense of the temporary is strong.

Our Times

The biblical words for time are worth examining. They help us in the short-term as well as in the long-term, as we seek 'to know our end and to be certified how long we have to live'.

To judge by the psalms, and much spiritual writing through the years, the times have persistently appeared uncertain, dangerous, and critical. We know the truth of this for individuals among our own acquaintance, for families, and for countries repeatedly disturbed, troubled, and distressed for varieties of reasons.

'God be at mine end' is a prayer about time, both the present and the future. That prayer can bring us through the day until bed-time and some sleep and rest, when we are weary and disconsolate. The same prayer can carry us through a crisis, as we look for a solution, a release from anxiety, an answer to a problem that is conclusive and satisfying. 'God be at mine end' on the lips of the young, or of a married couple on their wedding day, anyone at the beginning of a venture, is a prayer for a life-span.

In the language of the Scriptures, three meanings at least for 'time' can be usefully selected for our scrutiny and understanding.

First, 'time' may refer to the measurement of our life's duration. We number our days. We are conscious, too, that they are numbered.

We have clock-time and calendar-time. We sing 'Time, like an ever-rolling stream bears all its sons away.' If, as has been interpreted, the 'sons' are seconds, minutes, and hours, then we understand what follows: 'they fly forgotten, as a dream dies at the opening day.'

Secondly, another word for 'time' emphasises not 'duration' but a moment packed with event, a crisis that brings its demands for a decision or a message of judgment. This 'moment' can be an opportunity to affect a whole lifetime. In the twinkling of an eye, a whole period of time can be seen to have significance. A 'flash-back' reveals such turning points in time, which resemble the moment on the Damascus Road for Saul who became known as Paul, a moment that held a never-to-be-forgotten midday experience.

Thirdly, there is the longer view of time as 'era' or 'age'. Eternity or everlastingness was referred to poetically as 'ages of ages'. 'Our times' may stretch to the century's beginning, as we look back. The decade is taken as a measure by the planners as they work for the future.

We speak of the Christian 'era'. With the birth of Christ 'a new age' began, and with it 'a new order'. The poet Henry

Vaughan saw the great Christian event in terms not merely of 'era' but of 'eternity' when he wrote:

> I saw Eternity the other night
> Like a great ring of pure and endless light,
> All calm, as it was bright,
> And round beneath it, Time in hours, days, years,
> Driv'n by the spheres,
> Like a vast shadow mov'd; in which the world
> And all her train were hurl'd;

All three types of time claim our attention. It appeared to be a sign of special blessing, in the period of the patriarchs, such as Abraham, for a person to die 'full of days'. The short life of Jesus, however, packed with incident, clearly outstripped in significance and achievement the long lives of distinguished thinkers and leaders. Other short lives have been remembered for their lasting contribution to the welfare of humanity. Such fruitful careers, for all their brevity, have been said to have 'fulfilled many days'.

The kind of time which sums up in a moment a lasting achievement alerts the Christian 'to buy up the opportunity' while there is time, because the days are evil. 'Now is the time', 'it is high time to awake out of sleep', 'the hour is come', and many other calls underline the urgency of watchfulness and preparedness for much that is unpredictable in life. Sensitive timing in the witness and work of the Christian is all-important. 'There is a time to speak and there is a time to be silent' for those who are pledged never to be ashamed to confess the faith of Christ crucified. Our Lord's own example of eloquent silence at his trials reminds us that on occasions the time is not right for any speech or action on our part. The pain of doing nothing, yet patiently continuing at the ready, has to be endured at certain critical junctures.

We speak in paradoxical terms of 'making time' for others, 'finding time', or 'giving time', knowing that, while we have little control over the seasons and the years, we are still called to be responsible stewards of the lifetime allotted to us.

Those who have little to look forward to at the close of life take heart when they reflect that a golden opportunity of service may still be theirs, however weak or feeble the body may be. The unemployed, under the strains of redundancy, in the depressing search for a day's work, are faced with the grim alternative of 'killing time', unless a whole community of workers and workers alike, can combine to find fresh opportunities of service. A fellowship of suffering deserves creative thinking and ever further exploration in the face of the hard times of famines and destitution. For God to be included in these end-situations is the prayer of those who see work as service and love as sacrifice.

There is a wide sweep of prosperity and adversity when we look for the guidance of God through an era, an age, through our lifetime and on to the generation to come. One human life, with its before and after, is able to make only a very limited contribution to the stream of time. Each one is part of a tradition that moulds us and yet receives what we have to give as the years continue. We have received so much, consciously or unconsciously, from the heritage of the past that we cannot believe that any addition we may make to the sum total of our civilisation has any great influence or worth. We give what little we have contributed to God; he will grace it with a spirit that enlarges and transforms. In this way, the consecration of time turns life into vocation, in its widest sense of responsible calling, and interprets work as service.

The End is the Beginning

The Scriptures are reticent about the life beyond. The apocalyptic language of the last book of the New Testament is vivid and prophetic. Difficult to interpret, this vision in poetical language of rich and vivid imagery gives us few details about the nature of our destiny. On a broad canvas we see pictures of glory, praise, judgment, struggle with evil, and spiritual victory; God is Alpha and Omega, the beginning and the end. The one who makes all things new bringing hope for the future; a new heaven and a new earth.

The famous Saint Augustine helps us with words about 'the beyond'. In his *The City of God,* written at a time when the capital city of the great Roman empire has been sacked by invading Goths, he dares to sum up what we will have left to us in the end that is without end. The sack of Rome marked an end of an era. *The City of God* dealt with the contrast between Christianity and the world, and created new thinking out of a scene of destruction and despair. The Christian faith was challenged by the invader who also overthrew the city and shocked the civilised world at the time.

In terse terms, Augustine wrote of the future for Christians after death:

> we shall rest and we shall see;
> we shall see and we shall love;
> we shall love and we shall praise;
> behold, what will be in the end, without end.

These simple phrases contain a wealth of spirituality. Adaptable and flexible, they have brought comfort to many who either feared death or else refused to think about its inevitability.

'We shall rest' perhaps expresses the most common thought about the end of life. Many word-pictures have been painted of 'rest eternal', 'rest in peace', 'rest from labours', to give comfort and reassurance. This 'rest' tells only part of the story of the future. How does it match the visions of service or wider opportunity? How can his servants serve him in this atmosphere of rest, we ask.

'Rest' is to be distinguished from idleness and certainly from the boredom of passivity. Holding ourselves 'still' in the Lord can become 'recreation', which is a kind of rest. In quietness there is found a new confidence. The same Augustine confessed his earlier restlessness as he searched for answers to the questions which troubled him. 'Our hearts are restless until they rest in Thee;' this spiritual discovery became proverbial, when his own turbulent soul was laid bare through his description of his spiritual pilgrimage. 'Vacabimus' is the Latin word he used for 'we shall rest'. It suggests vacation. Here, at the end, there will be a clearance, so that life, uncluttered and unburdened, may continue with new vigour.

'We shall see.' Vision is another link in the chain of the experience he outlines. Much that had been hidden from our sight will be made plain. The contradictory and the inexplicable things of life on this side of the grave will have a fresh perspective. We have been obliged, in the nature of things, to see from our own end much that to us seemed baffling and indeed unjust and unfair. The Christian grave is a 'bed of hope': 'make us so to abound in sorrow for our sins', runs the old evening prayer, 'that when our bodies lie in the dust, our souls may live with Thee.'

Now we see through a glass, darkly, as it were, 'a dim reflection, in a mirror'; but, then, face to face, having 'crossed the bar'.

When we know 'as we are known' there is both joy and realism. To this we may look forward boldly. With this vision, we catch a glimpse of the meaning of life eternal described in the language of St John's gospel as 'knowing God'. There is a close link between 'knowing' and 'seeing'. If our sins are forgiven and our life is acceptable to God, entrusted to him, we find comfort and confidence in the beatitude: 'Blessed are the pure in heart, for they shall see God.' The visions of the young and the dreams of the old have introduced many to the glory that is in life and that shall be hereafter.

This is the vision splendid.

We shall see ourselves in a new light. We shall understand more clearly how we appear in God's eyes. Our life up to now has been spent groping in the gloom, in the semi-darkness of the twilight. Much has been obscured. We have often stood in our own light. In the end, we shall have that closer, personal view in his presence, when we shall see him as he is.

'We shall love' – with an everlasting love. The communion of saints is a holy fellowship marked by such a loving relationship. If we love God, we shall love others, too. This love must begin in us now. 'We ourselves have known and put our faith in God's love towards ourselves. God is love and anyone who lives in love lives in God, and God lives in him. Love will come to its perfection in us when we can face the day of judgment without fear; because even in this world we have become as he is.' (1 John 4:15).

We are not to think of the future entirely in terms of comfort or company. Yet the fellowship of the Church continues and offers us a life to share, a society to serve, and a sphere in which we can make a response to all that we receive.

We shall love God. This is our hope. We shall love him for what he is. We are his children, of his family. 'One family we dwell in him; one Church, above, beneath.' God is, by definition, Love. The Holy Trinity is not an abstract symbol for the indefinable. The association of persons in the fellowship of life expressed by that word, coined in faith and experience, is ever-living and ever-loving. We think, with the help of Augustine once more, of a Lover, a Beloved, and the abiding Love.

'We shall praise' brings us to a climax. This marks a fulfilment and an enjoyment beyond words. Praise cannot be narrowed down to songs of worship and the plucking of harp-strings. Praise fills every part of life with movement, service, faithful response, every possible attitude and activity which contribute to the showing forth of God's glory, not only with lips but in lives. This sort of praise, termed in one tradition 'an endless Alleluia' exceeds all earthly joy.

'Alleluia' is a shout of praise, filled with rejoicing and thanksgiving. It is an Easter word, and a stirring response to the greeting which announces that 'Christ is risen'. 'Praise the Lord' is its meaning. A shout of triumph, its significance needs to be constantly rescued from the vocabulary of formality and pious slogans. Christ's triumph is acknowledged, lest we ourselves become triumphalist. Resurrection life has endless resources for us to draw upon. The interaction of God and humankind, of spirit and flesh, provides many proofs that the world is God's world, a world over which he reigns with justice and with love.

That thought behind the shout of 'Alleluia' is never out of place. Nor has the praise of God ever sounded discordant amid all the changes and chances of Christian life. No matter how gloomy the times and evil the days in which we live, there is always a reason for praising God and rejoicing over what he has accomplished and still continues to bring about in us and our world.

Christ's appearances after his resurrection assure us of this. In those very scenes where there was the sadness of disappointment, where his friends felt that they had been failures, he brought answers of hope and delight. The sustained chorus of 'Alleluias' at the final scenes of the Passion play at Oberammergau sums up all that had been witnessed in the chequered story of love and suffering, sin and forgiveness, ruin and rescue so movingly dramatised. Handel's 'Hallelujah' chorus has a permanent place in the hearts of listeners, with its theme of victory over sin and death.

These shouts of joy renew human hopes over and over again. We begin to understand that the prayer of the Christian Church never ceases.

What is this 'prayer without ceasing?' We ourselves cannot pray all the time – in words, and yet more words. Prayer, of course, is a kind of life. There is a distinction between prayer and prayers. The words of praise or of helplessness, of joy or of bitter sorrow contribute to the life.

The prayers we offer may be other people's words borrowed or handed down, but they need not be outworn and lifeless because we have not originated them. We, on the contrary, can contribute to their meaning and help to keep them alive.

We should pray without ceasing, just because so many of our own efforts cease, peter out and collapse. Success is often temporary, hopes are dashed. Things apparently permanent become unexpectedly changed and disappear. Prayer expressing the love of God continues; a few faithful sustain its life. 'Someone has been praying,' we say, when we have faltered and yet have been supported unworthy as we are, in some crisis or misfortune.

Ultimately, to pray is to express love for God. Such love we withdraw at our peril. God does not cease to love us, through all our failings and faults. Perseveringly and unceasingly the selfishness of that constant inclination to claim, 'My will be done,' has to be transformed into 'Thy will be done.' This task is a life work, yet not a life sentence.

'Picture God as saying to you,' instructed Augustine, 'My son, why is it that day by day you rise and pray and bend the knee, and even sometimes shed tears, while you say to me, My Father, my God, give me wealth. If I were to give it to you, you would think yourself of some importance, you would fancy you had gained something very great. Ask of me better things than this, greater things than this. Ask of me spiritual things. Ask of me Myself.'